Training Manual for

the complete guide to
Godly Play

Jerome W. Berryman

An imaginative method for presenting scripture stories to children

© 2006 by Jerome W. Berryman

All rights reserved. No part of this publication may be reproduced or transmitted in any form or by any means, electronic or mechanical, including photocopy, recording, or any information storage and retrieval system, without permission in writing from the publisher.

The scripture quotations used in this work are from the *New Revised Standard Version of the Bible*. © 1989 by the Division of Christian Education of the National Council of Churches of Christ in the USA.

ISBN 978-1931960-25-0
ISBN 1-931960-25-9

TABLE OF CONTENTS

SACRED STORIES

Creation 5

The Exodus 13

The Ten Best Ways 21

The Exile and Return 29

PARABLES

The Good Samaritan 35

The Great Pearl 43

The Mustard Seed 51

The Sower 57

LITURGICAL LESSONS

Holy Baptism 64

The Good Shepherd and World Communion 71

The Circle of the Church Year 79

The Mystery of Easter 90

INTRODUCTION

We as Godly Play trainers are so pleased you have chosen to attend a Teacher Training Event. The time and effort you've set aside to become a better teacher reveals a deep devotion to the children in your faith community. As trainers we also know this action-reflection training provides an experience that not only immerses you in the stories, but helps you to understand Godly Play from the inside out.

Our publisher, Living The Good News, has prepared this training manual to accompany the Teacher Training Conferences. The manual is specially designed to enhance the training event. Lessons printed in the manual are copyrighted and are intended for training purposes only. You may have noticed that the booklet is bound so it will lay flat. Plenty of room is provided for you to personalize it with your own notes or diagrams. Use it to help make the stories your own. When you return home we hope you'll continue to use this valuable resource as you prepare to tell the stories to the children.

Perhaps you've already discovered that Godly Play really is "the best way" to help children enter the stories that are our heritage as Christians. The imagination of even the youngest child is captured by the words so carefully crafted and field tested over many years. Children first learn the stories with their bodies as they move the lesson pieces. Later they come to discover a rich and personal meaning that carries them though the places of danger, as well as provide entrance to places where there is good, green grass and cool, still fresh water.

It is our deep desire that through Godly Play your community will discover the power of stories to nurture the faith of each child. May God also bless each of you on your own faith journey.

SACRED STORY
CREATION

LESSON NOTES

FOCUS: THE DAYS OF CREATION (GENESIS 1:1–2:3)
- SACRED STORY
- CORE PRESENTATION

THE MATERIAL
- LOCATION: SACRED STORY SHELVES
- PIECES: 7 CREATION CARDS, DISPLAY RACK (OPTIONAL)
- UNDERLAY: BLACK FELT

BACKGROUND

With this lesson we begin to trace the elusive presence of the mystery of God in the story of God's People. We begin to play Hide-and-Seek with the Holy One and ask, "What can we know of the Giver by the gift?"

NOTES ON THE MATERIAL

This material sits on the top shelf of the sacred story shelves. The sacred story materials form a left-to-right sequence. For the sacred stories in this guide, the materials move from Creation to the Exile and Return. Thus the Creation material is found on the far left of the top shelf, the first material in the sacred story sequence.

A display rack holds up the seven cards so the children can see them. Also on the rack, in front of the upraised cards, is the rolled-up black underlay. This underlay is wide enough for all seven cards to be laid out side by side. The underlay is deep enough to place *two* rows of cards, one above the other. You can tape together a second set of cards to act as a self-checking set. When children work alone with the materials, they can compare their layout to the self-checking set to help them recall the order of days in creation. Store the self-checking set on a tray on the sacred story shelves, directly below the Creation material.

This lesson does not use a rug, since the material has its own underlay.

SPECIAL NOTES

At home: The days of creation make an especially wonderful story to share during a family vacation. For example, on the first day of the vacation you can lay out the first card and ask, "I wonder who saw light today?" When the family has finished sharing, you can give thanks to God for the gifts from creation you've enjoyed that day.

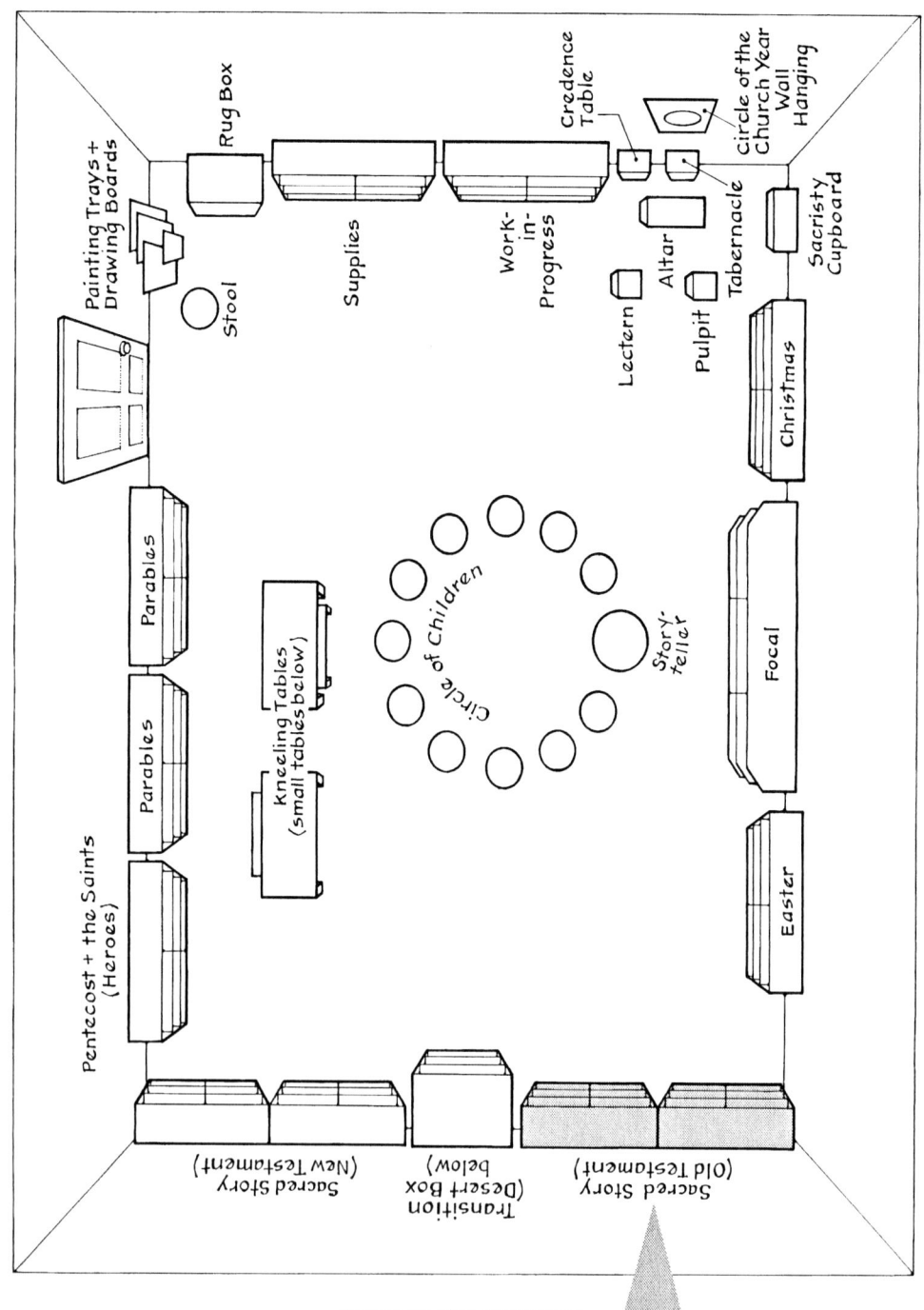

WHERE TO FIND MATERIALS

MOVEMENTS	WORDS
Move slowly and with deliberation to the shelf where the creation material waits.	Watch. Watch where I go.
Pick up the display rack for the creation lesson and return to the circle.	Do you see? Yes.

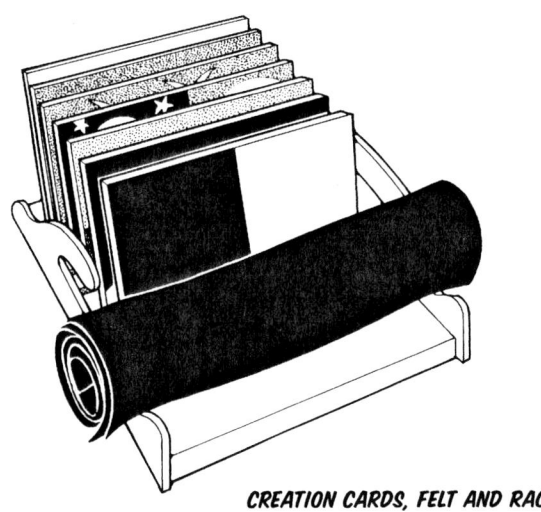

CREATION CARDS, FELT AND RACK

Place the rack beside you and get settled. Look around the circle. You may need to say:	Everyone needs to be ready.
Show the children how to "be ready" by sitting with your legs crossed and your hands relaxed on your ankles. Wait until all are ready.	
Look around the circle. Smile. Invite involvement by your own sense of openness. Wait. Nod your head, "Yes," as if someone is about to speak. The grand conversation has already begun!	What is the biggest present you ever got?

MOVEMENTS	WORDS
The children will begin to think of things they have received. They may begin with bicycles and video games, but they also may name something alive. If this happens, comment on the distinction between a gift that is inanimate and a gift that is alive. For example, you could say:	Listen. There's something different about that gift. (Wait to see if the children respond by describing the gift as alive. If necessary, describe that difference yourself.) That gift isn't like a bicycle. That gift is alive.
You are not saying whether living or nonliving presents are better. You merely notice the distinction for them to comment on if they wish. Continue to affirm the children's comments.	Listen. Listen to your friends. These are all big gifts. They are wonderful presents.
Whatever gift that a child names, unless you sense that the child is trying to shock or disrupt the group, is "wonderful." Continue the invitation to name greatest gifts until you think that all the children who want to speak have done so.	Yes. Yes. That is a wonderful present.
It is not a good idea to go around the circle one at a time, taking turns. Simply acknowledge each child when he or she is ready to speak. When all who want to speak have done so, then continue:	Did you know that there are some presents so big that nobody notices them? They are so huge that they are hard to see. They are so hard to see that the only way to know that they are there is to go clear back to the beginning, or maybe a little before the beginning.
Take the rolled-up black felt strip from the rack and place it on the floor to your right, so the children, who are facing you, will "read" the days of creation from left to right. As you speak, begin slowly to unroll the felt strip.	In the beginning...in the beginning there was... Well, in the beginning there wasn't very much.
When the strip is unrolled completely, you move your hand across its surface to show "nothing," moving from your right to your left, smoothing out the felt in one sweep.	In the beginning there was...nothing.

MOVEMENTS

From the children's point of view, you will now trace a "smile" from the children's upper left, down to the center and back up again to the children's upper right. (To you, these movements begin in the lowest right corner, move up to the center and end in the lowest left corner.)

Wait a moment and then take out the first card from the rack. This card shows the pictures of "light" and "dark."

Place the light card on the black underlay to your right so that the "dark" side of the card is closest to the right edge. Turn your hand so that the edge of your hand is perpendicular to the card and put it over the line between the light and the dark. Move your hand across the picture of light as you speak of that gift. When you name "light" or "dark," point to each.

WORDS

Except, perhaps, an enormous smile...but there was no one there to see it.

Then on the very first day God gave us the gift of light. So now there is not just darkness, but there is light and dark.

Now, I don't mean just the light in the light bulb or in the car lights at night. I don't mean just this light or that light, but I mean all of the light that is light. God gave us the gift of the light that all light comes from.

LIGHT AND DARK (STORYTELLER'S PERSPECTIVE)

As you say, "It is good," place your hand flat on the card, as if blessing it. This is probably the most important gesture in the whole lesson. Lean back, sit a moment and then begin the next day.

When God saw the light, God said, "It is good." And that was the end of the first day.

MOVEMENTS	**WORDS**
Place the second card to your left of the first day.	On the second day God gave us the gift of water. Now, I don't mean just the water in a water glass or the water in a bathtub or shower. I don't even mean just the water in a river or a lake. I don't even mean just the water in the ocean, or the water that comes down from the sky in rain. I mean all of the water that is water. This is the water that all the rest of the water comes from.
Move your hand across the card. You can trace the thin, white arc with your finger, or you can leave out this gesture and wait until the children ask about the line.	This is the firmament. It divides the waters above and the waters below.
Touch the card like a blessing.	When God saw the water, God said, "It is good." And that was the end of the second day.
Take out the third card and lay it to your left, so that it touches the second card. Take your time.	
Place the edge of your hand vertically on the card's line that divides the water and land as you say "divide." Move it to the right as you "uncover" the dry land. Point to the "green and growing things" on the card as you speak of them.	On the third day God gave us the gift of the dry land. God divided the water and the dry land, and gave us the gift of green and growing things.
Put your hand on the card like a blessing as you say, "It is good." Wait a moment. Enjoy all that was given on the third day.	When God saw the dry land and the green and growing things, God said, "It is good." And that was the end of the third day.
Take out the fourth card and place it to your left, so that it touches the card for day three.	On the fourth day God gave us the gift of the day and the night. God gave us a way to count our days.
Point to the lights as they are spoken of.	Here is the great light that rules the day, the sun, and here are the lights that rule the night, the moon and the stars.

| **MOVEMENTS** | **WORDS** |

Touch the card like a blessing as you say, "It is good." Wait a moment. Don't hurry. Enjoy the fourth day.

When God saw the day and the night, our way to keep time, God said, "It is good." And that was the end of the fourth day.

Take out the fifth card and place it to your left, so that it touches the card for day four.

As you mention the flying creatures and the swimming ones, touch each figure.

On the fifth day God gave us the gift of all the creatures that fly in the air. Not just the birds but all of the creatures that fly. And all of the creatures that swim in the water. All of them.

Touch the card like a blessing as you say, "It is good."

When God saw all of the creatures that fly and all of the creatures that swim, God said, "It is good." And that was the end of the fifth day.

Please remember to relax and enjoy each day after it is presented.

Take out the sixth card and place it to your left of the fifth one.

Touch the creatures as you name them.

On the sixth day God gave us the gift of all the creatures that walk upon the earth: the creatures that walk with two legs, like you and like me, and all the creatures that walk with many legs.

As you say "all the gifts of the other days," move your right hand over all of the card. Then touch the sixth card like a blessing as you say, "It is very good."

When God saw the creatures that walk with two legs and the creatures that walk with many legs and all the gifts of the other days, God said, "It is very good," and that was the end of the sixth day.

Take out the seventh card and place it to your left of the sixth one.

THE SEVEN CARDS (STORYTELLER'S PERSPECTIVE)

MOVEMENTS

As you say, "all the other days," sweep your hand across the whole line of cards.

Point to the seventh card.

As you say "mark it with a cross," you can use your fingers to trace a cross on the card. As you say "mark it with a star," you can use your fingers to trace the star of David on the card.

As you introduce the wondering questions, you can point to each card slowly as the question is introduced. For the last wondering question, you might pull one or two of the cards toward you so they are clearly out of line with the others. This is to suggest that these or others might be taken out for consideration.

When the wondering draws to a close, turn the children's attention toward getting out their own work.

You might also explore the sequence of the days. Can they be changed? The more years you present this story, the more powerful it becomes.

WORDS

On the seventh day God rested and gave us the gift of a day to rest—and to remember the great gifts of all the other days.

There is nothing here, because people go to different places to remember the great gifts. You can put something there to show your favorite place to remember. It might be in your backyard by a tree, in a church or in your room. It might be in the mountains or by the ocean or a lake. I don't know where your place is. Only you know.

What I do know is that this day is so special, that sometimes the Christian people mark it with a cross and the Jewish people mark it with a star, the star of David.

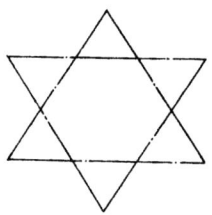

STAR OF DAVID

Now, I wonder which one of these days you like best?

I wonder which day is the most important?

I wonder which day you are in or which one is especially about you?

I wonder if we can leave out any one of these days and still have all the days we need?

SACRED STORY
THE EXODUS

LESSON NOTES
FOCUS: PASSOVER OF GOD'S PEOPLE (EXODUS 11:1–15:21)
- SACRED STORY
- CORE PRESENTATION

THE MATERIAL
- LOCATION: SACRED STORY SHELVES
- PIECES: DESERT BOX, PEOPLE OF GOD FIGURES, BLUE FELT, MATZO
- UNDERLAY: NONE

BACKGROUND

God was with the People as they "went out" (the literal meaning of the word *exodus*) from slavery into freedom through the water. The People of God have looked back to this time to sustain them when God is hidden and they feel lost. For the Jews, especially, the Feast of Passover keeps alive this core event. For Christians, Baptism reawakens this event, especially when commemorated in the Easter Vigil, celebrated on the eve of Easter by some denominations.

In these stories, we continue to evoke the People's experiences of God's elusive presence. These moments of high drama reveal the complexity of such experiences and provide a narrative of their richness. This not only gives children an appropriate language to name, express and value their own experiences but also permission to talk aloud about them.

NOTES ON THE MATERIAL

Locate the tray that holds this material on the sacred story shelves, to the right of the story of the Great Family as you face the shelves. On the tray, you'll find one basket that holds the People of God and two blue felt strips rolled up separately to represent the water. Also include a basket of *matzo*, the flat bread eaten by the Jewish People at the Passover. (From now on, have *matzo* available for children to eat, if they choose, each week.) Choose one figure from the People of God to represent Moses.

The basket that holds the People of God provides the people figures for several lessons that follow (the Ten Best Ways, the Ark and the Tent, the Exile and Return, etc.). In the story of Abraham and Sarah, the Great Family became present. God's People will now journey in the lessons as they do in fact—then, now and beyond. Therefore, keep plenty of small, wooden figures in this basket.

SPECIAL NOTES

Storytelling tips: When you prepare this story, you'll find that it "telescopes" or shortens the story of the journey into Egypt for food, omitting the details of the story of Joseph and his brothers (Genesis 42ff). The story of Joseph belongs in an object box, since it is about an individual's encounter with God rather than the People's encounter. You'll find more information about making and using object boxes on pages 22 and 72 in *The Complete Guide to Godly Play, Volume 1: How to Lead Godly Play Lessons*.

Another example of "telescoping," occurs during the narrative of the plagues. Rather than list the plagues—blood, frogs, gnats, flies, animals dying, boils, hail, locusts and darkness—we simply say "many strange things happened in the land," because the list often distracts children from the primary narrative.

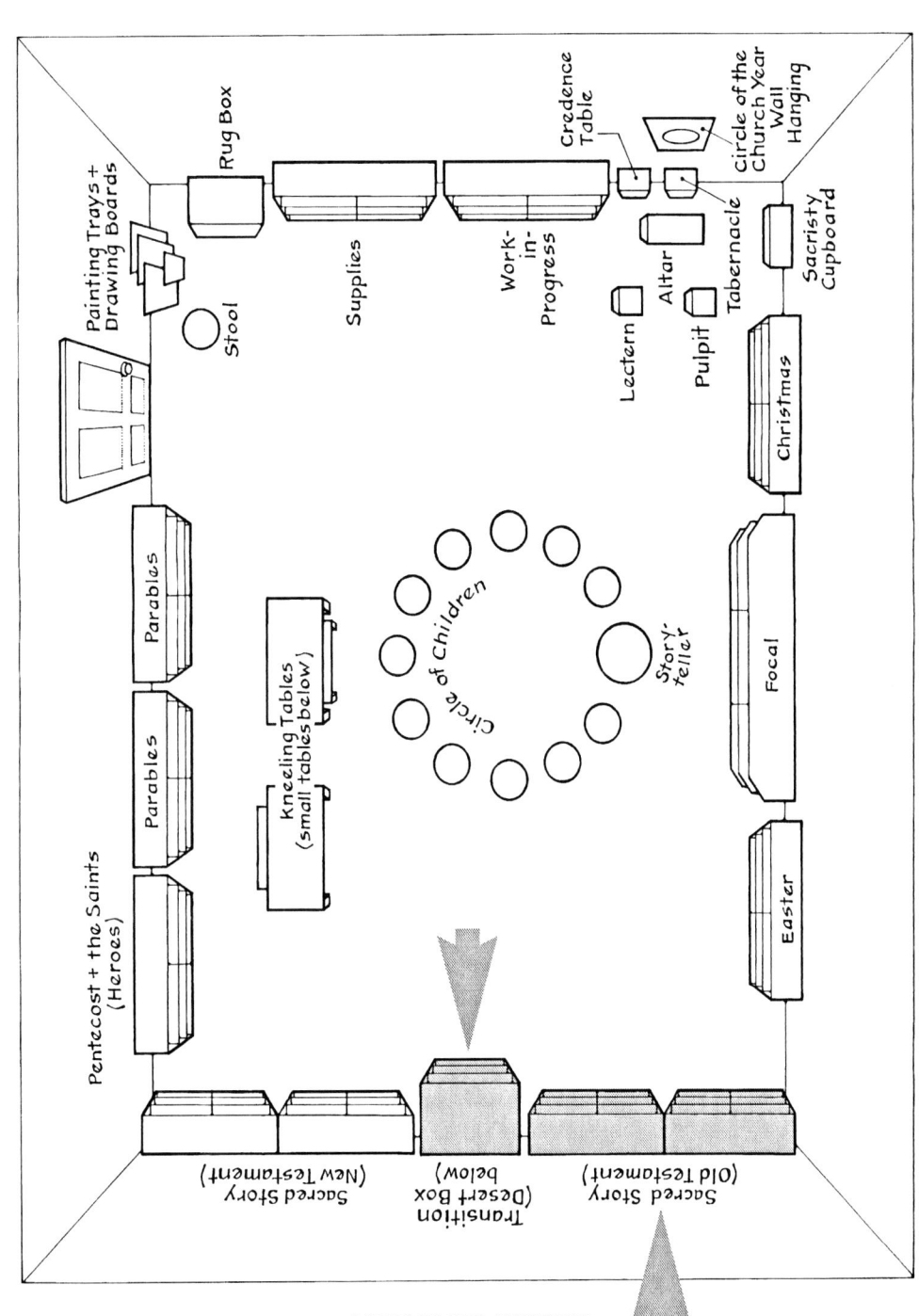

WHERE TO FIND MATERIALS

| **MOVEMENTS** | **WORDS** |

Go and get the desert box and bring it to the circle. Leave the cover on the desert box until you are ready to begin the lesson.

This lesson needs the desert box. Watch carefully, so you will always know where it is and how to get it out.

When you have the desert box in place, go to get the tray with the Exodus material.

Watch carefully where I go. Watch. Do you see the lesson? Here it is.

Bring the tray back to the circle and place it beside you. Now introduce the desert box to the children. This must be done carefully each time the desert box is part of a lesson.

This is the desert. It's not the whole desert. It is only a piece of the desert. We need part of the desert in our classroom, because so many important things happened there to the People of God.

Do not take off the lid until you are settled in the circle and the children are ready. The desert box is so exciting to some children, that you may want to wait to remove the lid until after you have introduced it.

The desert is a dangerous place. There is no food. There is no water. People die without food and water.

Remove the lid. Move your hand over the desert as you talk. When you mention how the wind changes the shape of the desert, take your hand and move the sand into new shapes.

Nothing grows there, so when the wind blows, the shape of the desert changes. People lose their way.

Take out some of the people and begin to place them in the sand to your left.

The desert is a dangerous place. People do not go there unless they have to. It takes courage to go into the desert.

Continue to put people in the sand as you tell about the need to leave Canaan and go to Egypt.

The People of God were living in a place where the rains did not come. The crops had no water, so they could not grow. There was no grain to grind to make bread. Everyone was hungry. The children cried in their sleep. So their mothers and fathers decided to go to a new land where there was food. They had to go even if it was across the desert. Their journey began.

Move the people across the desert, from left to right. Move them slowly, a few at a time, and reform the group several times on their way. Don't put more people into the sand than you can cover with two hands, because you will use that gesture when God's People become trapped.

It was hard in the desert, but they kept going toward the land called Egypt.

MOVEMENTS	WORDS
Move all the people to your right for their journey. This is because they will return in the next lesson from your upper right to your lower left, where you will place the rock for Mt. Sinai. When all the figures are in Egypt, pause.	In the land of Egypt the king was called a Pharaoh.
Put your two hands over the people with your fingers touching the sand.	When the people came into the land of Egypt, they found food and work, but the Pharaoh trapped them. They could not go home again. They had to do what the Pharaoh said. They had to live where the Pharaoh said. They had to get up when the Pharaoh said. They had to go to bed when the Pharaoh said. They had to eat what the Pharaoh said. They had to do the work the Pharaoh said. They had to do everything the Pharaoh said. They were slaves.
Remove your hands and put Moses in the sand close to you somewhere in the one-third of the desert box to your right.	One of the people, whose name was Moses, came to the Pharaoh and said, "Let my people go."
Each time the Pharaoh says, "No," hold your hand up flat between you and Moses. (You are taking the role of the Pharaoh in this dialogue.)	The Pharaoh said, "No." Moses went back many times to tell the Pharaoh to let his people go, but the Pharaoh always said, "No." Then many strange things happened in the land, but the Pharaoh always said, "No." Then something terrible happened. The oldest boy in each Egyptian family, even in the family of the Pharaoh, died. The oldest boys in the families of the People of God did not die, because the people made a mark on the doors of their houses. They put the blood of a lamb there, and the Angel of Death passed over them.
Hold out your hand again as if the Pharaoh is going to say, "No," but then let it crumple.	When Moses went back this time and said, "Let my people go," the Pharaoh said, "Yes."

Godly Play   The Exodus

MOVEMENTS	WORDS
	The people began to hurry to get everything ready. They packed all they could carry, and they baked bread for the journey. There was no time to put leaven in the bread and let it sit, so it would swell up and get big and fluffy like the bread you buy in the store. It was flat.
Show the basket of matzo to the children.	You can still eat this bread today. It is called *matzo*. Whenever you taste it, you can still taste this story.
Turn the people around and begin to move them from your right to your left. Move them about halfway across the desert box.	The people went as fast as they could. They were afraid the Pharaoh would change his mind. Suddenly they heard the sound they did not want to hear. The ground began to shake. The Pharaoh's army was coming after them. The beating of the horses' hooves, and the rolling of the chariots sounded like thunder!
Put down the two pieces of blue felt. They are of about equal length and meet in the middle of the desert box. Use your hand to suggest the "pushing" of the people "against" the water.	The army of the Pharaoh pushed the people against the water. They did not know what to do.
Fold each piece of felt back about an inch to make a passage through the water. Take the people through one at a time.	God came so close to Moses and Moses came so close to God that he knew how to take the people through the water into freedom.

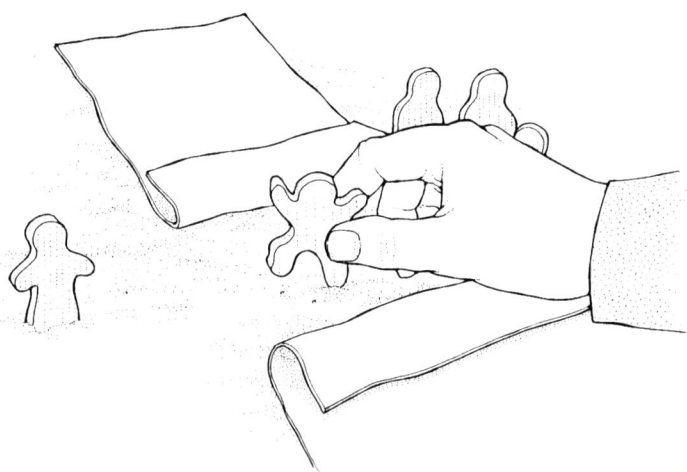

MOVING THE PEOPLE THROUGH THE WATER (STORYTELLER'S PERSPECTIVE)

MOVEMENTS

Look at the different figures and imagine how each one might feel. You might even say something like:

If there is time and the children are settled, you might pass around the basket of the People of God figures and have each child select one to bring through the water to the other side. Fold the felt back into the original position after all the people have passed through.

As the people come through the water to the other side, form them into a circle. Save one of the figures for Miriam. Place her in the center when the dancing begins.

WORDS

This one looks so scared he can barely move. This one is running. This one is happy. This one is confused.

When all the people were safe on the other side, the water closed behind them and they were free! The army of the Pharaoh could not get them.

Now all of the people were free on the other side. They were so happy they just had to give thanks to God, and Miriam led the dancing!

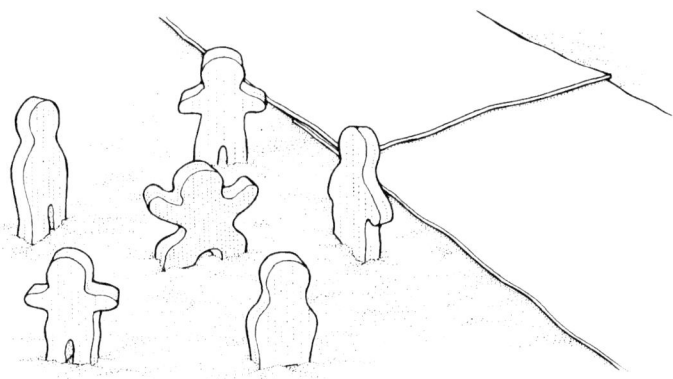

MIRIAM AND THE PEOPLE DANCE (STORYTELLER'S PERSPECTIVE)

Enjoy the story for a moment in silence. It is then time to begin the wondering.

I wonder what part of this story you liked best?

I wonder what part of the story is the most important?

I wonder what part of the story is about you or who you are in the story?

I wonder if there is any part of the story we can leave out and still have all the story we need?

MOVEMENTS	**WORDS**
When the wondering is drawing to a close, pick up the basket of matzos and show it to the children.	This is like the flat bread the people made so quickly. You can still eat it today. Whenever you taste this bread, you taste this story. This is the bread of the Passover Feast. It is called "matzo."
	I am going to pass it around. Every one of you may have a piece. Remember to wait to taste it until everyone is served. It is more fun to have a feast all together.
Help the children pass the basket around and support them while they wait. When the basket is all the way around, take matzo for yourself.	That's the way. You know how to do this. Good. That's right. We need to wait. Good. It is more fun to wait until everyone is served.
	Now let's enjoy the matzo all together. Taste the story. Taste how the people went through the water into freedom. You can almost taste the excitement.
	Yes. There is nothing in the bread except flour and water. They had to hurry. There is no leaven in the bread to make it get big and fluffy like the bread you buy in the store. This is unleavened bread. What you taste is the story.
	Watch carefully when I put this basket back. You can have all the matzo you want in our classroom. Remember to pass the basket around to everyone first. You also need to remember to taste the story.
	If the basket is empty, come and get one of the teachers to fill it.
Put the lesson back. Put the matzo basket on the shelf below it. Return the desert box to its place.	Now watch. I am going to put all of this lesson back.
Begin to go around the circle to help the children choose their work.	What work would you like to get out today?

SACRED STORY
THE TEN BEST WAYS

LESSON NOTES
FOCUS: THE TEN COMMANDMENTS (EXODUS 20:1-17; DEUTERONOMY 5:1-21)

- SACRED STORY
- CORE PRESENTATION

THE MATERIAL

- LOCATION: SACRED STORY SHELVES
- PIECES: DESERT BOX, PEOPLE OF GOD, HEART-SHAPED BOX WITH COMMANDMENTS, LARGE ROCK
- UNDERLAY: NONE

BACKGROUND

God was present to Moses at Sinai three times. First, God was present in the burning bush when God revealed to Moses the name of God (Exodus 3:1-6). Second, God was present when giving the Ten Commandments to the people through Moses (Exodus 19:18–20:1-17). Finally, after breaking the tablets in anger, Moses climbed up Sinai to receive the Ten Commandments a second time (Exodus 34).

On the last occasion, Moses bargained with God three times to see God's face (Exodus 33:12-14, 15-17, 18-22). But God did not allow this. No one could see God's face and live, so God put Moses in an opening in the rock and covered him until the dazzling light of God's presence had passed by.

NOTES ON THE MATERIAL

You'll use the desert box for this presentation. You'll also need the basket with the People of God figures from the Exodus story. You'll find the remaining materials—a heart-shaped box and a rock—to the right of the Exodus story materials.

In the heart-shaped box are three shapes (two tablets and a base piece) that fit together to form a heart shape. One tablet shape reads *Love God*. A second tablet reads

Love people. The third piece, the base piece, reads *God loves you*. There are also ten more tablet pieces, one for each of the Ten Commandments.

Each of the ten tablets are inscribed with a summary statement of one commandment. (See story for details.) Use dots on the back of the tablets—for example, two dots on the tablet with the second commandment—to organize this material more clearly. Finally, you need a large, rough rock to represent Mt. Sinai. To protect the wood of the shelf, place this rock on a cloth.

SPECIAL NOTES

Storytelling tips: We suggest that the story of Moses and the burning bush is part of the story of Moses' life, best told through an object box. You'll find more information about making and using object boxes on pages 22 and 72 in *The Complete Guide to Godly Play, Volume 1: How to Lead Godly Play Lessons*.

The story of the golden calf and Moses' third encounter with God are bracketed in the text for your convenience. Omit these sections, because they distract from the core narrative. However, if children ask questions about these details you will be ready to respond in narrative instead of with an explanation.

For three- to six-year-olds, use just the three summary tablets in telling the story: *Love God*, *Love people* and *God loves you*. Older children can hear all the commandments. From the age of nine and up, you can engage them in deeper discussion.

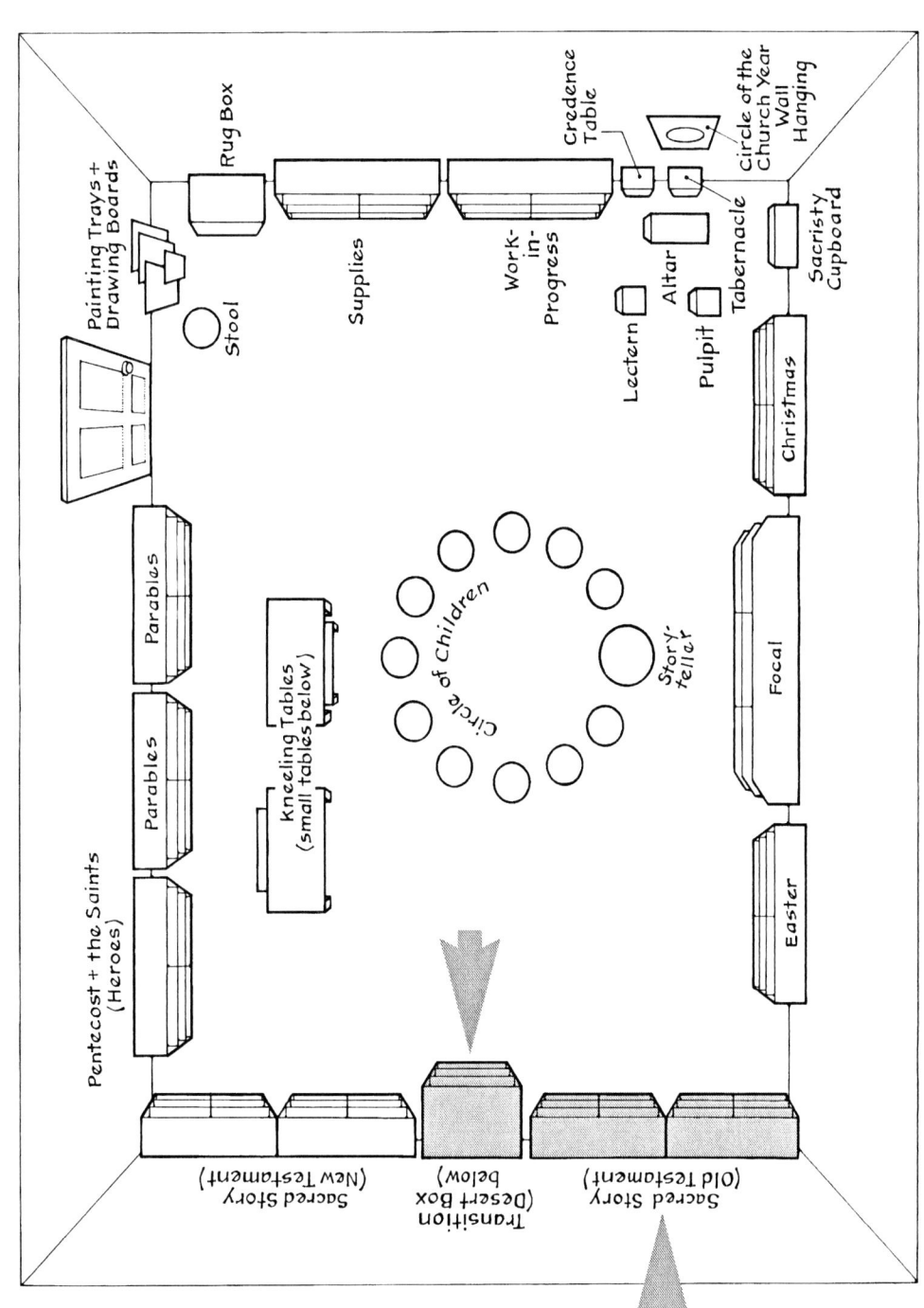

WHERE TO FIND MATERIALS

MOVEMENTS

Bring the desert box to the circle. Leave the lid on it. Go to the shelf and bring to the circle the People of God, Mt. Sinai and the heart-shaped box with the Ten Commandments.

Once you have the material assembled, sit and look at the desert box for a moment. If the children are comfortable and settled, remove the lid and begin the lesson. If they are not yet ready, leave the lid on and begin to talk about the desert box before removing the lid.

Put some of the people of God at your far right at the edge of the desert box. Arrange them in a circle. Also, place Mt. Sinai in the left hand corner of the desert box, the corner nearest you.

WORDS

Watch. Watch where I go to get the lesson. See? Here it is. Now you will always know where to find it.

This is the desert. It is a dangerous place. People do not go into the desert unless they have to. There is no water there, and without water we die. There is no food there. Without food we die.

When the wind blows, it changes the shape of the desert. People get lost. Some never come back.

In the daytime the sun is so hot that people must wear lots of clothes to protect themselves from the sun and the blowing sand. The sand stings when it hits your skin. The sun scorches you by day. At night it is cold. You need many clothes to keep warm. The desert is a dangerous place. People only go there if they have to.

The people of God went through the water into freedom. They were free, and Miriam led the dancing!

Now that the people are free, they can go anywhere they want to go and do anything they want to do. Where will they go now? What is the best way?

THE PEOPLE OF GOD IN THE DESERT (STORYTELLER'S PERSPECTIVE)

MOVEMENTS

Show the heart-shaped box as you say this, but don't open it yet.

Begin to move the people to your left. Mt. Sinai is in the lower left corner of the desert box, closest to you, so that most of the children can see what happens. If you put it in one of corners closest to the children, it will block the view of many of the children. Move the People carefully until they are all at the foot of the mountain.

Move Moses up to the top of the rock. As he moves up the mountain, hide the figure in your hand to show his disappearing in the smoke.

Move Moses down the mountain, revealing him from your closed hand, and place him in the sand.

[If you choose, you can add this bracketed part of the story. There is no need to make a golden calf. The children can use their imaginations to complete the scene.]

WORDS

God loved the People so much that God showed them the Ten Best Ways to Live. Sometimes these ways are called the Ten Commandments.

As the people traveled across the desert, they followed fire by night and smoke by day. They began to complain. Some even wanted to go back to Egypt. There was not enough food. There was not enough water. God helped Moses find food and water. Finally they came to the great mountain.

The People came close to the mountain, but they were afraid to touch it. Mount Sinai was covered with fire and smoke. Moses was the only one who had the courage to climb up into the fire and smoke to meet God.

When Moses was on top of the mountain, he came so close to God, and God came so close to him, that he knew what God wanted him to do. God wanted him to write the Ten Best Ways to Live on stones and bring them down the mountain to the People.

God gave the Ten Commandments to Moses. Moses gave them to the people and they gave them to us.

[The first time Moses was on the mountain, the people grew tired of waiting for him to come back. They wanted a god they could see, so they melted all of their gold and molded a golden calf to worship as if it were God. When Moses saw the idol they had made and the people dancing around it, he was angry. He threw down the two tablets of the law and broke them.]

[The next day Moses said to the people, "You have sinned a great sin." He told them that he would climb the mountain again. Perhaps God would forgive them if he went back.]

[When Moses was on the mountain, he wanted to come even closer to God's presence. He wanted to see God's face. "Show me your glory," Moses said. God said, "You cannot see my face and live."]

MOVEMENTS

[Place your hand, palm down, hiding Moses.]

When the commandments are finally presented to the people, begin to lay them out. Begin first with the summary. One tablet says, "Love God." The other one says, "Love People." A third triangular piece completes the shape of a heart, and says, "God loves us." As you lay these pieces flat in the sand, read them aloud:

Sometimes with three- to six-year-olds, it is good to stop with the summary and skip ahead to the wondering questions. With older children, you can move through all of the commandments.

As you read each of the commandments, place that tablet upright in the sand with the writing facing the children. A small number or row of dots on the backs of the commandments will guide you during the discussion.

The way the commandments are laid out is significant. There are the ones for being close to God, and the ones for being close to people, and there is one for both. It stands in the sand between the other two categories.

Place the first three tablets in a line, upright in the sand next to "Love God." Read each slowly.

WORDS

[God put Moses in a cleft of the rock and put his hand over him to protect him from God's presence. God took away the hand, after passing by, and Moses saw God's back.]

[Meeting God face to face is sometimes too much for us. When we see God's back, we can follow God all our days.]

Love God. Love people. God loves us.

1. Don't serve other gods.
2. Make no idols to worship.
3. Be serious when you say my name

MOVEMENTS	**WORDS**
Read the fourth tablet and place it in a middle position in the sand since it tells us how to love both God and people.	4. Keep the Sabbath holy.
Read the next tablets slowly and place them next to "Love People." Say each one with kindness and understanding. After reading #7 you may want to say, "You know, when people get married they think they will be married forever. Sometimes it just doesn't work out."	5. Honor your mother and father. 6. Don't kill. 7. Don't break your marriage. 8. Don't steal. 9. Don't lie. 10. Don't even want what others have.

THE TEN BEST WAYS TO LIVE (CHILDREN'S PERSPECTIVE)

I know. These are all hard. God did not say that these are the "ten easy things to do." They are the Ten Best Ways to Live, the Ten Commandments. They are hard, perhaps even impossible, but we are supposed to try.

They mark the best way—like stones can show the right path.

MOVEMENTS

WORDS

Important discussions can arise from each of the "best ways" or commandments. Take your time. Wait, so children can raise issues and misunderstandings. With children about the age of ten, you may want to put two commandments such as "Honor" and "Do not lie" side by side in the sand and ask how you can keep both if Mommy or Daddy ask you to tell a lie. Another suggestion is to ask how we can keep "Do not kill" and stay alive? Almost everything we eat is alive from chickens and cows to carrots and lettuce.

When the discussion quiets down, you can begin the wondering.

I wonder which one of the Ten Best Ways you like the best?

I wonder which one is most important?

I wonder which one is especially for you?

I wonder if there are any we can leave out and still have all we need?

When the wondering about the Ten Commandments is finished, turn back to the whole story. The story can get lost as the wondering about the Ten Best Ways takes place. It is now time to put all of that discussion back into the context of how God loves us so much that God gave us the Ten Best Ways to Live.

Now, let's go back again to the story. I wonder what part of the whole story you like best?

I wonder what part of the story is the most important?

I wonder where you are in the story or what part of the story is about you?

I wonder if there is any part of the story we can leave out and still have all the story we need?

When all the wondering is finished, put the materials away and invite the children, one by one, to get out their work.

SACRED STORY
THE EXILE AND RETURN

LESSON NOTES

FOCUS: GOD'S PRESENCE WITH THE PEOPLE IN EXILE (2 KINGS 25; 2 CHRONICLES 36:13-23; EZRA; NEHEMIAH)

- SACRED STORY
- CORE PRESENTATION

THE MATERIAL
- LOCATION: SACRED STORY SHELVES
- PIECES: DESERT BOX, PEOPLE OF GOD, CHAIN, BLUE YARN, BLOCKS
- UNDERLAY: NONE

BACKGROUND

Abraham and Sarah traveled away from their home, a land where people thought that gods were in each thing—such as in the sky, in a river or in a tree. The understanding that all of God might be everywhere sustained Abraham and Sarah as they finally made their way to Canaan, where Laughter (Isaac) was born. And God was there.

In this lesson, nearly the same arcing journey is taken by God's People, but this time in the opposite direction. Even though this journey is forced onto God's People, the same astounding discovery is made. God was not just in one place, in the temple in Jerusalem. God was also in a foreign and strange land. God's presence is not here or there, but everywhere, waiting. To be found. To find us.

NOTES ON THE MATERIAL

Use the desert box for this lesson. Locate the tray with material for this lesson on the top shelf of the sacred story shelves, to the right of the Ark and the Temple as you face the shelves. The most important item is a large chain, long enough to stretch from one side of the desert box to the other. Keep the chain in its own basket on the tray so the children can see it and wonder about it as they look along the shelves.

The tray also holds two pieces of blue yarn for the Euphrates and Tigris rivers, a block of wood to represent Haran and a larger block of wood to represent the city of Babylon, which was in fact contained within a square system of walls. You will also need several People of God figures.

SPECIAL NOTES

Storytelling tip: The People of God figures are in the basket with the Exodus material. For many of these sacred stories for Fall, you have used some of these figures. Using the same figures emphasizes that the "same people," that is, the People of God, have made this journey together, seeking the elusive presence of God.

The children also have to work out among themselves how they will share the People of God.

In this lesson, we return to using the desert box. Remember to begin the lesson by first introducing the desert box. When children are settled, you can remove the lid from the desert box. Find guidelines for helping children get ready in a circle—or helping them get ready again, after an interruption—on page 69 in *The Complete Guide to Godly Play, Volume 1: How to Lead Godly Play Lessons.*

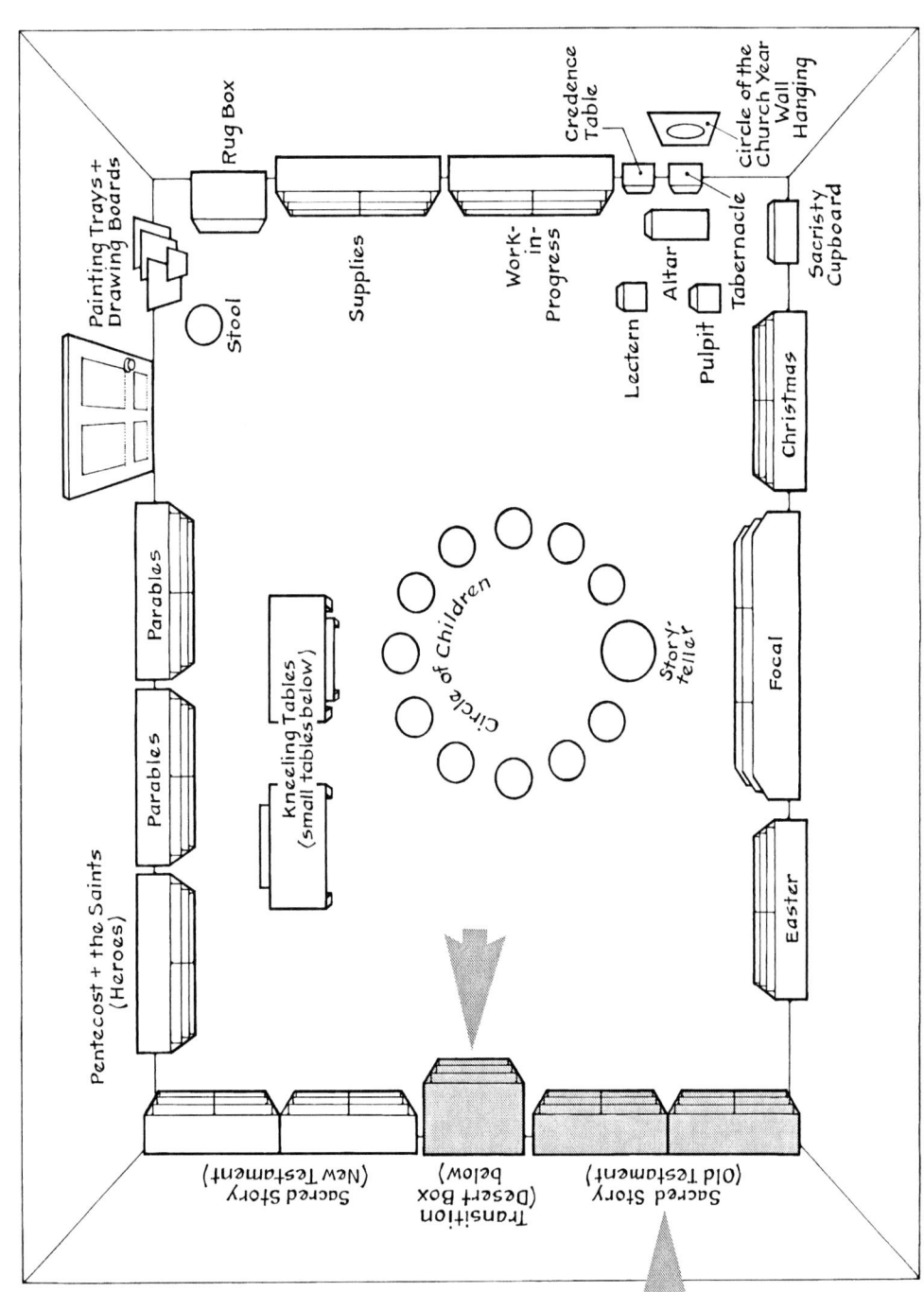

WHERE TO FIND MATERIALS

MOVEMENTS	WORDS
When the children are settled, bring the desert box to the circle. Leave the lid on it. Go to the shelves and return with the tray for the Exile and Return. You will also need some People of God figures from the Exodus basket.	Watch where I go to get this lesson.
If the children are ready, remove the lid to the desert box and begin to tell about the desert. If they are not quite ready, leave the lid on and begin to tell about the desert before removing it.	This is the desert. The desert is a dangerous place. There is no food or water there. People can die in the desert. When the wind blows, the shape of the desert changes. You can lose your way. The sun is so hot that people wear many clothes to keep the sun from burning their skin. When the wind blows, the sand stings your face and hands. People need protection from the blowing sand. At night, it is cold, and you need many clothes to keep warm. The desert is a dangerous place. People do not go there unless they have to.
As you begin to introduce the story, mark in the sand a square about five inches on each side in the corner of the desert box on your far right, closest to the children. Put several of God's People inside the square. This represents Jerusalem. Also mark in the sand a similar rectangle inside "Jerusalem" to represent the temple.	This is Jerusalem. Here is the wall. Inside is the temple built for God. Here are the People of God. They knew that God was in the temple, but they also thought that it was the only place where you could pray to God.
Place a block of wood in the center of the box, close to you, to represent Haran. Place a larger block at your far left to represent Babylon. Place two pieces of blue yarn at the left to represent the Tigris and Euphrates rivers.	People thought that the wall of the city would protect them from everything.
Move your hand from your left to right across the desert, since the Assyrians came from the East.	Then came the Assyrians, and they attacked the city. It was a terrible time. People fought, and some starved to death. Finally, the Assyrians went away.
When the Babylonians take the city, brush the sand to erase parts of the lines to show destruction.	Then the Babylonians came, and they did not go away. Their king wanted the city of Jerusalem for himself. They broke down the walls and burned the temple.

MOVEMENTS

WORDS

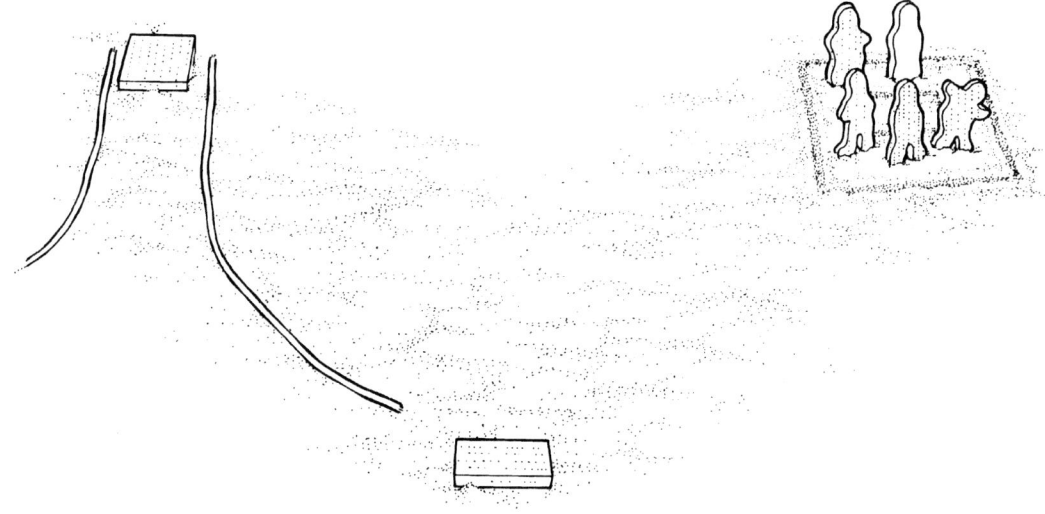

THE PEOPLE OF GOD IN JERUSALEM (STORYTELLER'S PERSPECTIVE)

Leave a few people in the city and begin to move the other figures away.	They took many of the people away. Only a few were left in the land.
Move the people from your right towards you and then down to your far left along the Euphrates river to Babylon. Move the figures slowly, only a few steps at a time for each figure.	The soldiers marched God's people away from Jerusalem. They looked back at the smoke of the burning city and wondered if they would ever see it again. As they walked through the desert, they had to get up when the soldiers said. They had to eat what the soldiers said. They had to go where the soldiers said. They had to go to bed when the soldiers said. They grew weary, and some died. It took a long time.
When the people pass Haran, pick up the large chain and drop it across the middle of the desert box between the people and Jerusalem. Listen to the terrible sound of the metal chain striking the sand.	They were in exile. They could not go home.
As the people approach Babylon you tell of their sadness.	They hung their harps on the weeping willow trees and sang sad songs. They dreamed of Jerusalem and the temple, but they could not go back.
Turn the figures to face toward Jerusalem.	They even faced towards Jerusalem when they said their prayers.
	Slowly, God's people began to understand that God was in this place, too. God's presence came to them as they gathered to read the scriptures, to tell the old stories and to pray

Godly Play   The Exile and Return   33

MOVEMENTS

WORDS

The king of Babylon allowed many of God's People to work. They set up little stores, and some worked for the king. It was a shock when the king of Persia came with his army and took Babylon for himself.

When the people begin to return to Jerusalem, march them back the way they came and have them climb slowly over the chain, one at a time. When they "rebuild" the temple, make the mark in the sand distinct again.

This new king began to let some of the people go back to Jerusalem. Some went with Ezra. They began to rebuild the temple.

Move two or three people back the way they came and have these figures, too, climb over the chain.

More were allowed to go back. They went with Nehemiah. They rebuilt the walls around the city.

Pick up the chain and place it on the tray.

Then the People of God were no longer in exile. They could go home again. Do you know what happened? Not all of them went home.

Move your hand over the whole desert.

Now they knew God was in the strange and foreign land. Some stayed, because God was there, too.

Enjoy the story for a moment in silence. It is then time to begin the wondering.

Now I wonder what part of this story you like best?

I wonder what part is most important?

I wonder where you are in the story or what part of the story is about you?

I wonder if there is any part of the story we can leave out and still have all the story we need?

When the wondering is finished, put the lesson back on the shelf. Put the desert box back in its place. Re-turn to the circle and begin to help the children decide what work they are going to get out that day in response to the lessons and issues they need to work on.

PARABLE OF
THE GOOD SAMARITAN

LESSON NOTES

FOCUS: THE SAMARITAN AND THE WOUNDED TRAVELER
(LUKE 10:30-35)

- PARABLE
- CORE PRESENTATION

THE MATERIAL

- LOCATION: PARABLE SHELVES
- PIECES: PARABLE BOX WITH DARK BROWN DOT, LIGHT BROWN FELT ROAD, 2 BLACK FELT PIECES, 2 CITY SHAPES, 6 PEOPLE (1 INJURED PERSON, 2 THIEVES, 1 PRIEST, 1 LEVITE, 1 SAMARITAN), 1 "COVERING PIECE" (A PICTURE OF THE SAMARITAN HELPING AN INJURED PERSON)
- UNDERLAY: BROWN BURLAP

BACKGROUND

This parable is found only in Luke 10:30–35. The lawyer's question about the greatest commandment which frames the parable also appears in Mark (12:28–34) and in Matthew (22:34–40), but without the Samaritan.

NOTES ON THE MATERIAL

Find the material in a gold parable box with a dark brown dot, located on the top shelf of one of the parable shelves. Inside the box is a brown underlay, rough and irregularly shaped. There is a lighter brown strip for the road and two black pieces of felt, one for each side of the road. At each end of the road is an abstract city. The outline of Jerusalem has the temple in its appropriate place.

The figures you will use include the person who was injured, the two thieves, the priest, the Levite and the Samaritan. One additional item is called the "covering piece"; it is a picture showing the Samaritan with his donkey as the Samaritan puts a coat on the injured person. This piece is large enough to cover the two figures used on the road. You will place the covering piece over the Samaritan and the injured person, then move the Samaritan and the hurt person together with this covering piece toward Jericho.

SPECIAL NOTES

Classroom Management: The violent events of this parable can sometimes disturb children. Di Pagels, an experienced Godly Play storyteller, recalls a time when one boy turned to another and pushed him hard, saying, "That's what *I'd* do." Instead of focusing on the child's disruption, Di paused in her storytelling, raised her eyes to all the children and said, "I wonder how it felt for that man to be hurt by the robbers." She gave the boy and the entire group an opportunity to enter with more empathy into the feelings of the wounded, and the disruption passed.

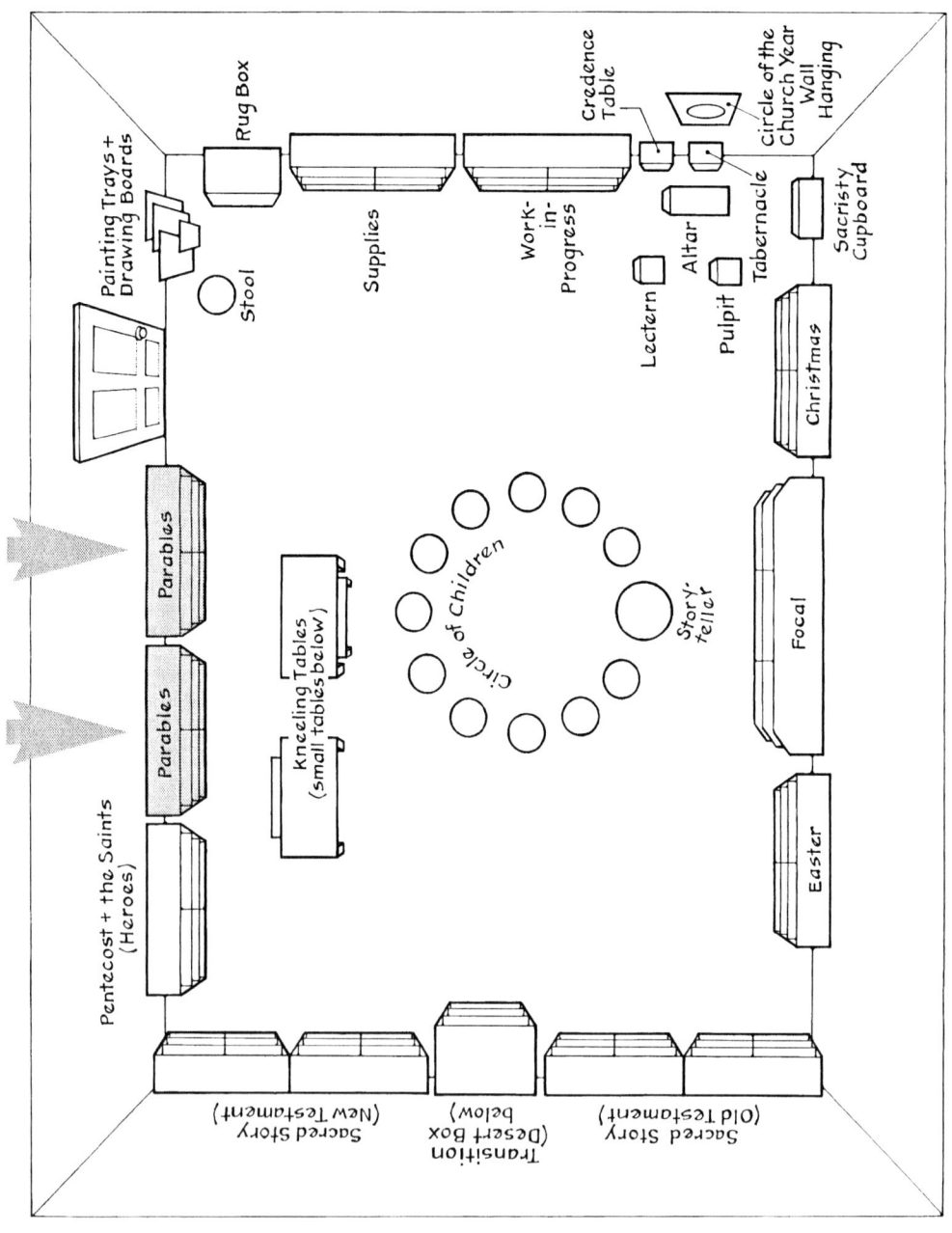

WHERE TO FIND MATERIALS

MOVEMENTS

WORDS

Go to the parable shelves and pick up the gold parable box. Point to the dark brown circle on the box, which signifies that this is the parable of the Good Samaritan.

Watch carefully where I go so you will always know where to find this lesson.

Bring the box to the circle and place it in the middle of the circle. Sit back, and begin when you and the children are ready.

You need to be very careful when you come close to a parable. You need to be ready. You can break a parable if you aren't ready.

Look. The box is the color gold. Perhaps there is something valuable like gold inside. There could be a parable inside. They are very valuable. They are worth even more than gold.

Knock on the top of the box as if the top were a door.

The box also has a lid on it. Sometimes it is as if parables have doors that are shut. You can't go inside the parable even if you are ready. I don't know why. It just happens, so don't be discouraged. Keep coming back again and again. One day the parable will open up for you.

The box looks like a present. You know, there may be a parable inside, because you were given parables as a present, even before you were born. Even if you don't know what a parable is, it is still yours.

Sit back again. Continuing reflecting on what might be in the box.

It looks old. Parables are also old. They are older than you, and they are older than me. They are even older than your grandmother or grandfather. They are almost two thousand years old.

Move the box to your side and take the lid off. Lean the lid on the side of the box toward the circle so the children cannot see into the box. This increases the mystery and decreases the distraction of what is about to come out of the box for most of those in the circle. You may need to ask the child sitting next to the box if it will bother him or her to have it there. They sometimes begin to announce what is coming, which breaks everyone's concentration.

I wonder if there really is a parable inside? I have an idea. Let's look and see.

Hmmm. I wonder what this could be?

MOVEMENTS

Remove the brown underlay. Drop it in a crumpled shape in the middle of the circle and look at it for a moment. Then, begin to smooth it out.

Wait for the children to begin to wonder. If they do not begin, you might suggest a few things like a giant cookie or a piece of wood to get them started. See if you can leave dirt or the desert for them to propose. If there is silence, let there be silent for awhile. It is important for the children to know that silence is important and no cause for anxiety.

Wait a moment and then turn to the box and bring out the "road." Lay the road from one corner to the other, starting at your near left.

The children may see the new piece as a road or a river. It might be a fence you have to jump over. (Move your fingers along and jump them over it.) There are many things it might be. Invite the children to help you build the metaphor of the parable so it will be the common property of all.

Place Jerusalem and then Jericho at opposite ends of the road. Make sure Jerusalem is at the end nearest you.

Take the two black pieces of felt from the box one at a time. Put one on one side of the road and the other on the other side of the road at the midpoint of the road.

WORDS

I wonder what this could really be? There is so much brown. There is no green at all. Look, there is no blue. There is nothing but brown, and the brown is scratchy.

It is hard to know what this could really be if there is only brown. Let's see if there is anything else in the box that can help us.

Now, I wonder what this could be? What could it really be? Yes. It could be a crack. Perhaps the whole thing is going to break into two pieces?

Let's see if there is anything else to help us. Oh, look. It is a road. It is going from this place to this place. But there is more. Look at this.

I wonder what these could be? There is no light in them at all. They are like shadows. Let's see what else there is to help us make the parable.

38   *Parable of the Good Samaritan*   *Godly Play*

MOVEMENTS	WORDS

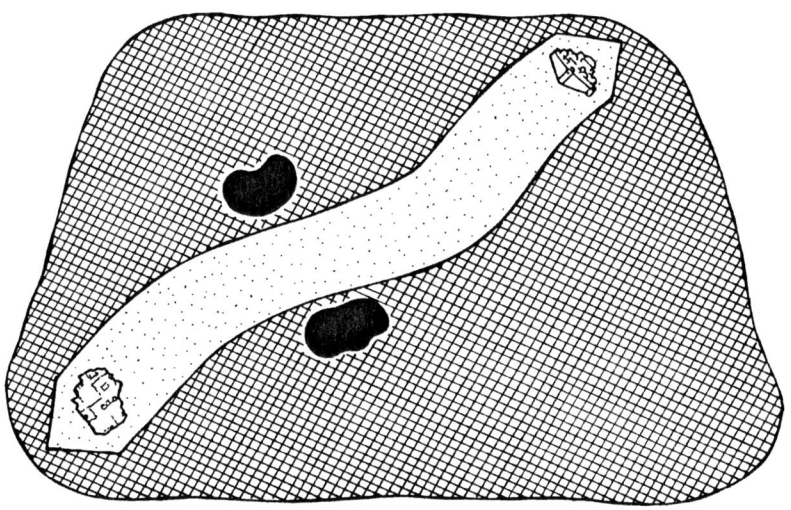

JERUSALEM AND JERICHO (STORYTELLER'S PERSPECTIVE)

Take out the two thieves and put one behind each of the black felt pieces by the road. Sit back and prepare. When you and the children are ready, you begin.	
	There was once someone who did such amazing things and said such wonderful things that people followed him. As they followed him they heard him speaking of many things. Sometimes people asked him questions.
	One day a person asked him what the most important thing in life is. The person he asked said, "You already know."
	"That is true. I do. It is to love God and to love people just like they are your neighbors." The person paused a while and thought. He then asked another question, "But who is my neighbor?"
	The person he asked then told this parable.
Take the person out of the box who is making the journey and place him at the Jerusalem end of the road by you. Begin to move him slowly along the road, toward the children, as you speak.	There was once someone who went from Jerusalem down to Jericho. As he went along his way he was attacked by robbers. They hurt him, took everything that he had, and left him by the side of the road half dead.

Godly Play   Parable of the Good Samaritan

| **MOVEMENTS** | **WORDS** |

Take the robbers out from behind the "rocks" and placed them in an "X" over the traveler. Then move the robbers off the underlay, back to the box or to your side. When you say "half dead" you turn over the traveler. He is at the side of the road by one of the "rocks."

Move the priest from Jerusalem slowly down the middle of the road. Don't hurry.

There was also a great priest of the temple who went on the road from Jerusalem down to Jericho. As he went along his way he came to the place where the person was who had been hurt, had everything taken from him, and had been left by the side of the road half dead.

When the priest comes to the injured traveler, move the priest slowly to the other side of the road and past the traveler. When the priest is past, move him back into the middle of the road and on to Jericho. Move the priest off the underlay.

When the priest came to him, the priest went to the other side and went along his way.

Move the Levite slowly down the road. When he comes to the injured traveler, move the Levite to the other side of the road and past the traveler. When the Levite has passed the traveler, move him back into the middle of the road and off the underlay.

There was also someone else who worked at the temple who went from Jerusalem down to Jericho. He was one of the people who helped the priests. He took care of the temple and helped with the music. He was called a Levite.

When the Levite came to the place where the person was who had been hurt, had everything taken from him, and been left by the side of the road half dead, he went to the other side, and he went along his way.

Move the Samaritan slowly down the road until he comes to the injured traveler.

There also was a person who went on the road who did not live in Jerusalem. He was visiting from a country called Samaria. The people in Samaria did not like the people in Jerusalem, and the people in Jerusalem did not like the people from Samaria.

Move the Samaritan to the traveler.

When the stranger came to where the person was who had been hurt, had everything taken from him, and had been left by the side of the road half dead, the stranger went to him.

MOVEMENTS

Then reach into the box and take out the "covering piece" that shows the Samaritan putting a coat on the injured traveler. Put the card over the figures of the Samaritan and the traveler.

WORDS

The stranger put medicine on the places where the person was hurt. He gave him his coat to put on. He then put him on his donkey and took him to a place to spend the night.

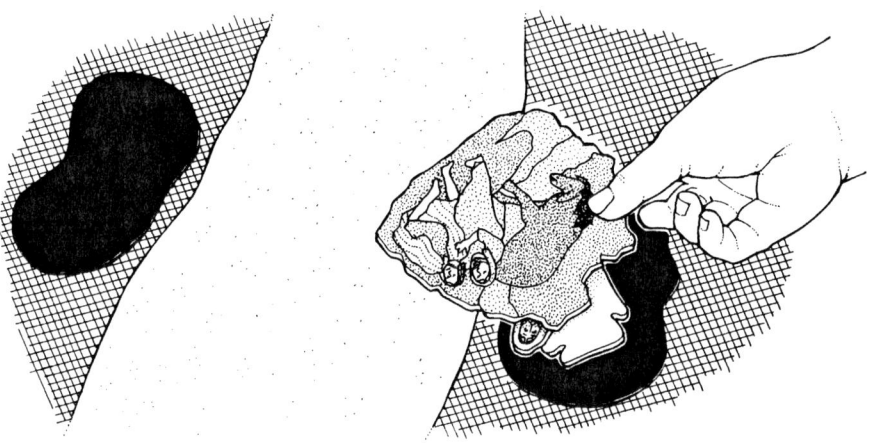

PLACING THE "COVERING PIECE" (STORYTELLER'S PERSPECTIVE)

Move the stranger and the traveler with the card over them along the road almost all the way to Jericho.

The stranger even stayed with him all the night, and in the morning he gave the innkeeper enough money for him to stay there until he was well.

Sit back and ponder the whole parable. While you are doing this, line up the figures to your left on the underlay closest to you. Put the traveler farther away from you and the other figures, but also on the underlay. You are going to place different figures beside the traveler and ask who is the neighbor.

Now I wonder, who is the neighbor to the person who was hurt, had everything taken from him, and was left by the side of the road half dead?

Place the priest beside the traveler. Ask the first question. Wait. Repeat for the Levite and the thieves. Finally place the Samaritan. The children may disagree, but usually there is no question about who the neighbor is. You then go on.

I wonder if it could be this one? This one? Could it be this one? I wonder if it could be this one?

Godly Play   *Parable of the Good Samaritan*   41

| **MOVEMENTS** | **WORDS** |

Move the traveler to join the other figures at your near left. Put one of the robbers in the place where the traveler was. Move the priest up beside the robber. Try the Levite. Some may have already asked you to try the other robber. The Samaritan needs to be tried. The one that may create the most discussion is the traveler.

I wonder who is the neighbor to this one? Ahh. That's not so easy, is it? Could it be this one? How about this one? This one?

Move the priest down to the comparison position. Some will think the Levite has to be his neighbor since he works for him. Much discussion will follow.

Who is the neighbor to this one?

Try different combinations of the figures, always asking:

Who is the neighbor to this one?

When you have tried all of the combinations of the figures, turn to this final bit of wondering. All of the figures are still laid out on the underlay.

Now I wonder what would happen if the people in the parable were women and not men?

When the wondering about the change of men to women begins to subside, wonder about children. The children need to know that going to get help is also helping.

I wonder what would happen if the person finding the injured traveler were a child?

Pick up each figure, one at a time, and carefully place them back in the box. Put the road and the dark pieces in the box, then fold up the underlay and place it in the box, too.

Here is the traveler.
The Samaritan.
The priest.
The Levite.
The two thieves.
The rocks.
The city and the inn.
The road.

Walk slowly to the parable shelves and return the parable box to its proper place. Help the children decide what work they will get out during the response time.

Now watch carefully where I go, so you will always know where to get this parable.

PARABLE OF
THE GREAT PEARL

LESSON NOTES

FOCUS: THE MERCHANT AND THE GREAT PEARL (MATTHEW 13:45)
- PARABLE
- CORE PRESENTATION

THE MATERIAL
- LOCATION: PARABLE SHELVES
- PIECES: PARABLE BOX WITH WHITE DOT, 5 BROWN RECTANGULAR PLACES, 2 FIGURES (MERCHANT AND SELLER), MERCHANT'S POSSESSIONS (MONEY, CHEST, BED, CANDLE, VASE, CHAIR, FOOTSTOOL)
- UNDERLAY: WHITE

BACKGROUND
In the canonical gospels, this parable is found only in Matthew 13:45. Another version of the parable can be found in the Gospel of Thomas (Gospel of Thomas, 76).

NOTES ON THE MATERIAL
Find the material in a gold parable box with a white dot, located on the top shelf of one of the parable shelves. Inside the box is a white underlay in the shape of a circle. There are two figures, the seller, shown sitting at a table, and the merchant.

Five brown, felt rectangular "outline" shapes of various sizes represent houses, villages, countries, worlds—living places or other realities. These shapes are empty, with an opening in each one. Inside one shape, place the seller at a table.

Inside another outline shape, place an assortment of goods: a bed, a chest, bags of gold, chair, footstool, a candle, a vase and other things. These are the possessions which the merchant will exchange for the great pearl.

A little gold box contains three pearls, each one a different size. (Placing cotton in the box helps show that the pearls are important.) As you lay out the story, you will place one pearl on the table in the seller's place and two other pearls in two of the remaining empty shapes. One outline shape remains entirely empty.

SPECIAL NOTES

Storytelling Tip: When you tell the story, you may be tempted to use the largest pearl for the great pearl. Choose a different pearl instead, because greatness has to do with more than size. Be prepared for the children's wondering to touch upon this issue. Children often regard big things as more important than small; for example, they might feel that adults are more important than children. Furthermore, our culture holds up big things for us to admire, too, from big houses to big cars and big bank accounts.

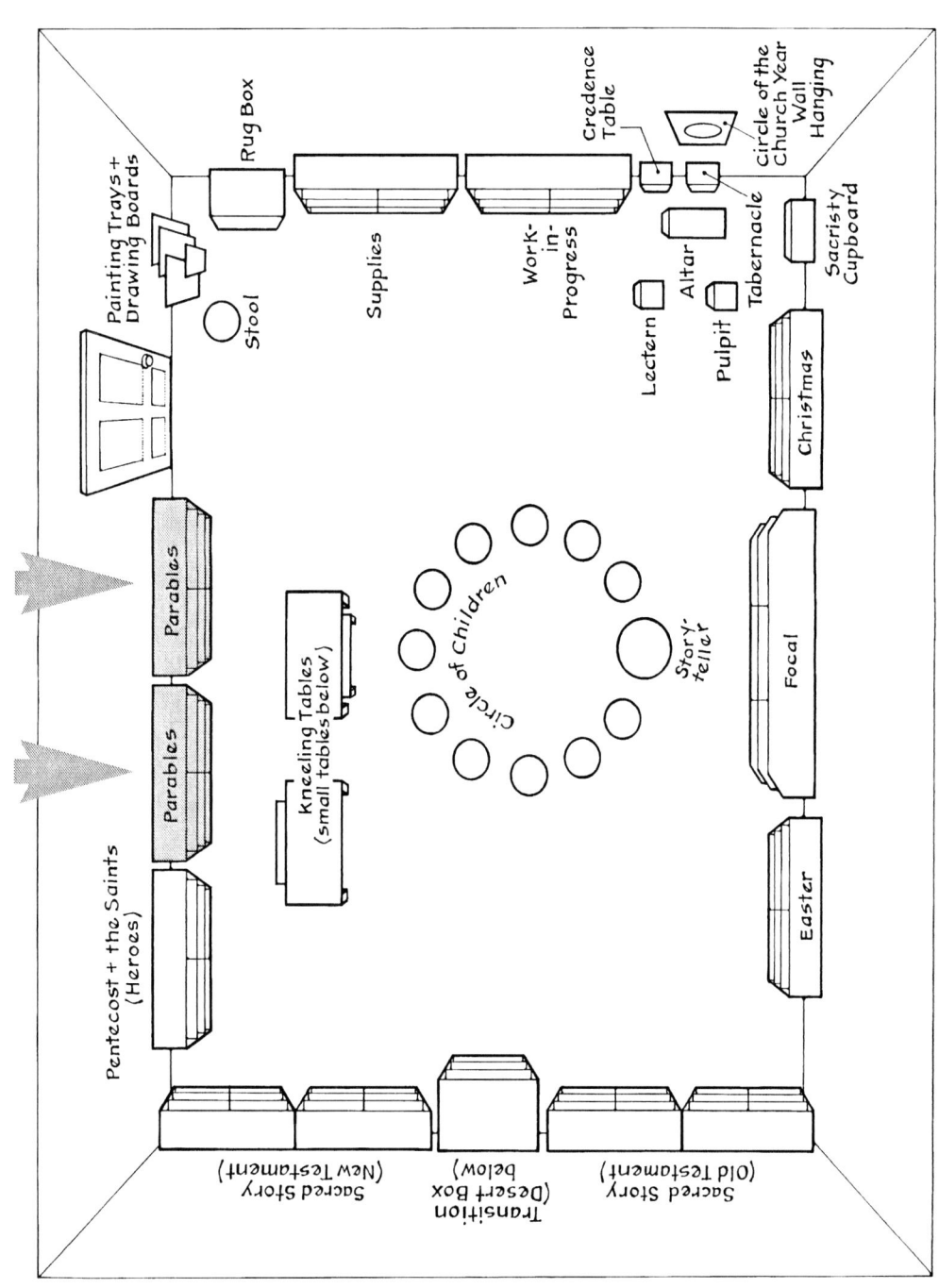

WHERE TO FIND MATERIALS

MOVEMENTS

Go to the parable shelves and pick up the gold box with the white dot on it. Point to the dot, but you do not need to say anything about it.

Carry the box to the circle of children. Place it in the center of the circle. Touch it with pleasure and interest as you introduce the material to the children.

Move the parable box from the middle of the circle of children to your side. Remove the lid and lean it against the side of the box between the box and the children. This helps the children keep focused on what is already laid out and not worrying about what is coming next. It also keeps some of the mystery of the parable box in place.

Take out the underlay. Leave it crumpled in the middle of the circle for a few moments as you begin wondering what it could really be. As you continue wondering, smooth it out.

WORDS

Watch carefully where I go so you will always know where to find this lesson.

I wonder if there could be a parable inside this box? It is the color gold. There must be something important inside. Parables are very important, so maybe there is one inside this box.

Parables are very old, and this box looks old. Perhaps there is an old parable inside.

Did you know that parables were given to you before you were born? This box looks kind of like a present. Parables are presents, so maybe there is a parable inside this box.

Look at this lid. Sometimes parables have a lid on them, like a door that is shut. The lid keeps you from going inside the parable. I don't know why. This sometimes happens even if you are ready, so don't be discouraged. Keep coming back to the parable, and one day it will open up for you.

I have an idea. Let's look inside this box and see if there is a parable there.

Look at this. It is something. I don't know if it is a parable or not. Well, at least we can see that it is very white. Everywhere there is anything, it is white.

I wonder what this could really be? Yes, it looks like a snowball. It is cold. I wonder what else it could be? Could it be the moon, I wonder? I wonder what this could really be?

MOVEMENTS

When the wondering about the underlay is almost finished, take out the brown rectangular pieces one by one. You will not be able to tell which one you have because they are crumpled. Take them out at random. This helps your own sense of the parabolic. You will have a different configuration, something unsuspected, every time.

Put your finger on a corner of the figure and pull one of the sides from that point. Place your finger at the next corner and pull the next piece out to its length. Do this for each brown piece. This is a way to organize the setting up of the figures and it helps smooth them out. Place each brown piece at a different place on the underlay.

Place the merchant and the contents of his house in one of the brown rectangular figures farthest from you. Those contents include: bags of money, chair, a chest, candle, his bed, and other household or personal items. Place the seller and his table in the large brown figure that is closest to you. You will have three empty figures.

Take out the little gold box with the pearls inside. Let it sit for a moment and then open it with mystery. Silently place a pearl on the table in front of the seller. Put one pearl in two of the three empty rectangular figures.

WORDS

I wonder what this could be? It is brown, but what could it really be in the parable?

Hmmm. This is strange. I wonder if they fit together?

Oh, this helps.

Let's see if there is anything more inside the box to help us.

No. There is nothing else. All we can do now is begin.

MOVEMENTS

WORDS

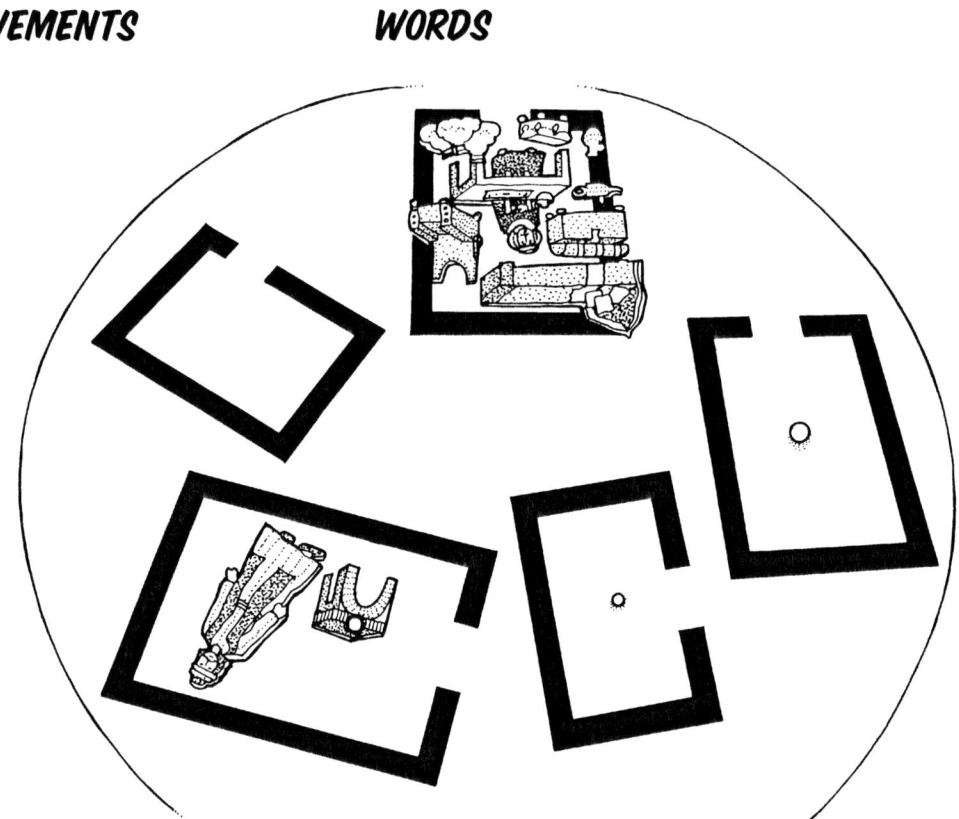

THE PARABLE OF THE GREAT PEARL (STORYTELLER'S PERSPECTIVE)

Sit back for a moment. Reflect silently on all that is laid out before you on the underlay. Wait until you are ready. If they need it, help the children get ready.

There was once someone who said such wonderful things and did such amazing things that people followed him. As they followed him, they heard him talking about a kingdom, but it was not the kingdom they lived in. It was not like any kingdom they had ever visited. It was not like any kingdom that they had ever even heard of.

They couldn't help it. They had to ask him what the kingdom of heaven was like. One time when they asked him, he said, "The kingdom of heaven is like when a person who buys and sells fine pearls, a merchant, goes to search for the great pearl."

Move the merchant out of his home's doorway and let him stop briefly at each of the other places (the brown outline shapes). Pick up the pearl when there is one there and hold it up close to your own eyes (for the merchant) and inspect it. Put it back and

48 *Parable of the Great Pearl* Godly Play

MOVEMENTS	**WORDS**

shake your head. It is not the great one. Finally, the merchant comes to the place where the seller is sitting behind a table. On the table is the great pearl. Pick it up and nod your head yes.

The merchant leaves the pearl on the table of the seller. He goes to his home and brings the bags of money.

"When he found the great pearl, he went..."

He goes back and returns with the chest. He brings the chair, the vase, the candle...everything but his bed. Finally, he goes to get the last piece inside the house, which is his bed. He then returns to his house, folds it up and places it inside of the seller's house.

"...and exchanged..."

The merchant then goes back to where his house once was. Leave him there with the pearl, sitting right in the middle of his former home. Place the pearl at the center of the merchant.

"...everything for the great pearl."

There is, of course, silence during the movements of the merchant. Don't hurry. Acknowledge the questions of the children as well as their exclamations. Don't stop until you finish the sentence with the phrase "everything for the great pearl."

Sit back and rest for a moment before you begin the wondering. Prepare for your own wonder. It has to come from within you to be real.

I wonder if the person was happy with the great pearl?

I wonder what the merchant is going to do now?

I wonder why the seller was willing to give up something so precious?

I wonder if the seller was happy with all of his things?

I wonder if the seller has a name?

MOVEMENTS

WORDS

I wonder if the merchant has a name?

Now, I wonder what the great pearl could really be?

I wonder what could be so precious that a person would exchange everything for it?

I wonder if you have ever come close to the great pearl?

I wonder where this whole place could really be?

When the wondering concludes, put the pieces of the parable back carefully into the box. Don't hurry. Name each one as you put it away.

Here is the great pearl.
Here are two other pearls.
Here are all the merchant's new things.
Here are the places.
Here is the seller, and here is the merchant.

Return the parable box to the shelves and go back carefully to the circle. Sit down to help the children decide what work they are going to get out.

PARABLE OF
THE MUSTARD SEED

LESSON NOTES

FOCUS: THE MUSTARD SEED AND SHRUB (MATTHEW 24:32; MARK 4:30-32; LUKE 13:18-19)

- PARABLE
- CORE PRESENTATION

THE MATERIAL

- LOCATION: PARABLE SHELVES
- PIECES: PARABLE BOX WITH YELLOW DOT, GREEN FELT SHRUB (OR TREE), GOLD BOX WITH BIRDS AND NESTS, FIGURE OF A PERSON
- UNDERLAY: YELLOW

BACKGROUND

This parable is found in all three synoptic gospels and in Thomas (Matthew 24:32; Mark 4:30–32; Luke 13:18–19; Gospel of Thomas 20). The mustard in the parable is not the domestic mustard we use for flavoring. The mustard of the eastern world grew and spread quickly. Farmers did not like it because it could take over a field and ruin its useful production of grain. It is a shrub and not a tree. These historical matters are not interesting to children, but they are mentioned to invite the reader to discover more about this parable as an adult.

NOTES ON THE MATERIAL

Find the material in a gold parable box with a yellow dot, located on the top shelf of one of the parable shelves. The underlay is yellow and shaped with the top a bit wider than the bottom. The sides are curved like a seed. The shape suggests a seed and more. There is a green shrub or tree made of felt to be unrolled. Birds and nests are kept in a separate small gold box with a lid. Finally, there is the figure of a person who puts the tiny seed in the ground.

SPECIAL NOTES

Tip: Why tell parables? In parables, we enter with wonder to live the question. Parables question our everyday view of life. They wake us up to see in life what we have not seen before. Parables question the status quo, the order imposed by tradition, power or class. That is why Jesus' parables often got him into trouble, and why Christians ever since have sometimes redefined parables in ways that comfort us *only* rather than challenge us by disrupting our comfortable worldviews.

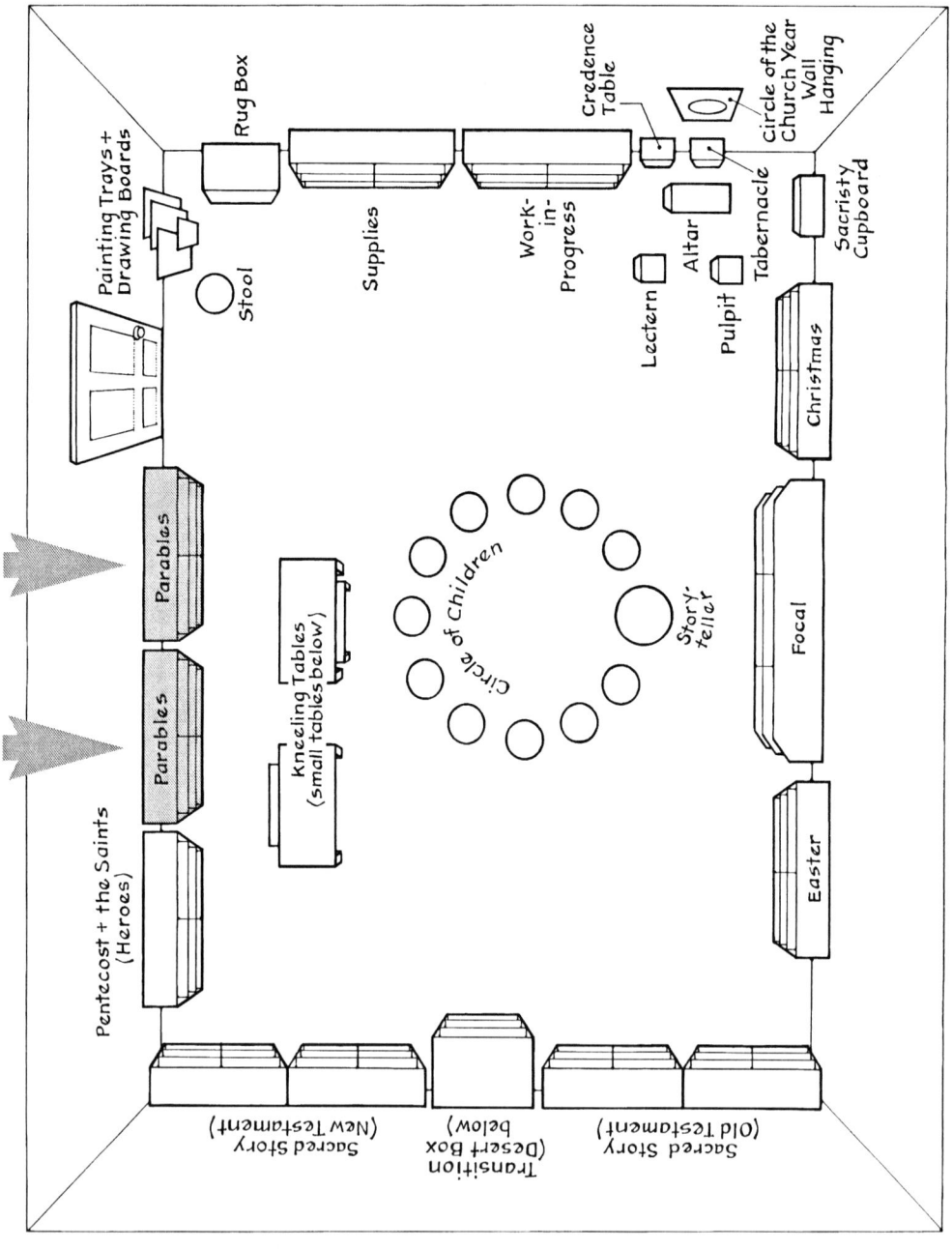

WHERE TO FIND MATERIALS

MOVEMENTS	*WORDS*

Go to the parable shelf and pick up the parable box with the yellow dot on it. Point to the dot, but do not say anything to the children. Bring the parable box to the circle of children and place it in the middle. Sit down and become comfortable.

Watch where I go to get this material.

As you speak, pick up the box and look at it more closely.

This box looks old. Parables are old. I wonder if there is a parable inside?

Trace the outline of the box as you speak about its color and value.

The box is the color gold. Parables are valuable, maybe even more valuable than gold.

Knock on the lid, like knocking on a door, when you note the difficulty of entering parables at times.

Look, the box has a lid. I know, boxes have lids, but so do parables. Sometimes, even if you are ready, you cannot enter the parable. The lid is like a door. Sometimes it is closed. If that happens don't be discouraged. Come back to the parable again and again. One day it will open for you.

Hold the box out like a present.

The box looks like a present. Parables are presents. They were given to you before you were born. Even if you do not know what a parable is, it has still been given to you.

When several or all of the introduction sentences are finished, sit for a moment. Let your authentic interest and love of parables be apparent.

I know what let's do. Let's look inside to see if there really is a parable there. I know they are easy to break, so let's be careful.

Move the box from in front of you to your side. Remove the lid and lean it on the box so the children will not be distracted by looking inside. This also helps maintain a sense of mystery.

Take out the underlay and leave it for a moment crumpled in front of you. Then begin to smooth it out as you talk.

I wonder what this could be? I wonder if it could be a parable? It is certainly yellow.

Hold your hand a few inches above the underlay. Push your hand down into the "color" that is there. Imply that the "yellow" has substance to it beyond the cloth. Invite the children to play with the idea of what the underlay could be.

There is nothing else here but yellow. I wonder what this could really be? Yes, I know it does look like a lemon.

I know, it could be the sun. I wonder what else it could really be?

MOVEMENTS

WORDS

Take out the rolled up green felt tree and hide it inside your closed hand. While you are hiding it, keep eye contact with the children so they will look at you rather than at the material.

A lemon drop? I wonder.

Look carefully into the box. There is nothing there to help get ready. The pieces left all have to do with the telling of the parable.

Let's see if there is anything else in here that can help us get ready.

Oh no, there isn't anything else! All we can do is begin.

There was once someone who said such wonderful things and did such amazing things that people followed him. As they followed him, they heard him speaking about a kingdom, but it was not like the kingdom they lived in. It was not like any kingdom they had ever visited. It was not even like any kingdom anyone had ever heard of.

They couldn't help it. They had to ask him. What is the kingdom of heaven like? One time when they asked him that he said, "The kingdom of heaven is like when a person..."

Take the person figure from the parable box. Place it at the edge of the underlay farthest from you, facing the children. The shrub will be planted there and grow "up" (from the children's perspective) toward you.

Hold up your closed hand that contains the "tree" and cover it with your other hand. Extend the first finger of the closed hand to show that you cannot see the seed. This kind of mustard seed comes in a pod and the individual seeds are like dust. You really could not see it.

"...took the tiniest of all the seeds, a grain of mustard seed, a seed so small that if I had one on my finger you would not be able to see it."

Put your finger down into the underlay to plant the seed close to the farthest edge.

"The person put the tiny seed in the ground, and it began..."

54 *Parable of the Mustard Seed*

| **MOVEMENTS** | **WORDS** |

Inside your closed hand is the felt tree, so when you say "grow" you can begin to unroll it. Unroll it all the way to its top and then begin to extend the branches that were folded first, the last time you put the parable away.

"...to grow."

Take the small gold box out of the parable box. Set it down on the underlay. Do not hurry. Remove the lid. Take a few of the birds out of the box, one at a time. Place them flying toward the tree.

"The shrub grew up so big it was like a little tree, and the birds of the air came..."

Take a few other birds from the box, one at a time, and place them around the tree. Take a few nests from the box, and place them in the branches of the tree.

"...and they made their nests there."

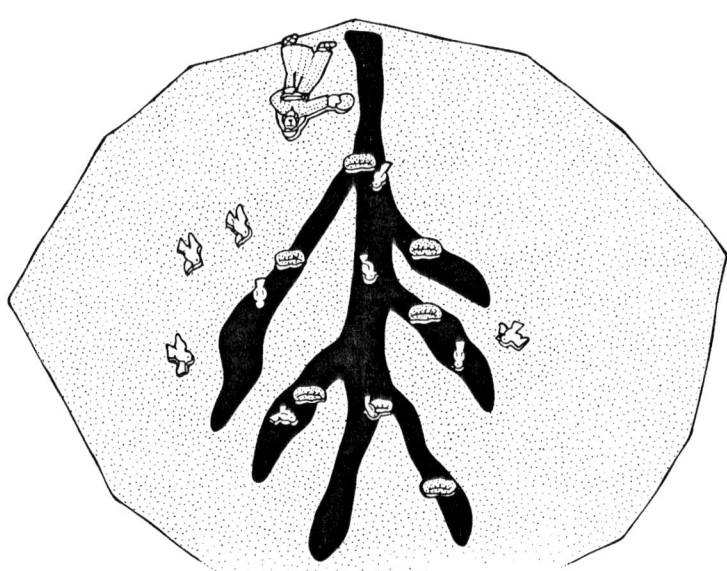

THE PARABLE OF THE MUSTARD SEED (STORYTELLER'S PERSPECTIVE)

Sit back and enjoy the birds and the tree. If the children are well settled, you might pass around the box of birds and nests and invite the children to put birds and nests in places that are just right for them.

MOVEMENTS

When you are finished with the birds and nests, it is time to begin the wondering.

WORDS

Now I wonder if the person who put the tiny seed in the ground has a name?

I wonder if the person was happy to see the birds coming?

I wonder what the person was doing while the shrub was growing?

I wonder if the person could take the shrub like a tree and push it all back down inside the seed?

I wonder if the seed was happy while it was growing?

I wonder where the seed was when it stopped growing?

I wonder if the birds have names?

I wonder if they were happy to find the tree?

I wonder what the tree could really be?

I wonder if you have ever come close to this kind of tree?

I wonder what the nests could really be?

I wonder where this whole place could really be?

When the wondering draws to a close, begin to place the birds and nests back into the little box first, and then put the rest of the objects into the parable box itself. While you are putting things away, you might name the things again. This also is a good time to ask the children to begin to think about what work they will get out during the response time. The underlay goes in last.

Take the parable box back to the parable shelves, return to the circle and begin to help the children decide what work they will get out.

PARABLE OF
THE SOWER

LESSON NOTES
FOCUS: THE SOWER AND THE SEED (MATTHEW 13:1-9)
- PARABLE
- CORE PRESENTATION

THE MATERIAL
- LOCATION: PARABLE SHELVES
- PIECES: PARABLE BOX WITH LIGHT BROWN DOT, GOLD BOX OF BIRDS, 3 EARTH IMAGES (ROCKY SOIL, THORNS, GOOD EARTH), 3 BAGS OF GRAIN, 1 SOWER
- UNDERLAY: LIGHT BROWN

BACKGROUND
This parable is found in all three synoptic gospels and in the Gospel of Thomas (Mark 4:1-9; Matthew 13:1-9; Luke 8:4-8; Gospel of Thomas 9). The parable, which describes Jesus' promise of abundant harvest, is followed by an allegory that expresses the concerns of the first century Church.

NOTES ON THE MATERIAL
Find the material in a gold parable box with a light brown dot, located on the top shelf of one of the parable shelves. The underlay is a long strip of brown. There are three individual pieces with images representing the rocky soil, the thorns and the good earth. As you tell the parable, lay out the matching image for the kind of soil being described.

Three bags of grain, in increasing sizes, represent the harvests of thirty, sixty and one hundred measures. There is also a little gold box full of birds and the figure of the sower.

SPECIAL NOTES

Storytelling Tip: You'll find the introductions to each parable very similar. You need not repeat the words exactly the same each time, but do try to make your introductions similar. This repetition serves in the same way as the phrase "once upon a time" in many stories. Familiar words signal something out of the ordinary is about to happen.

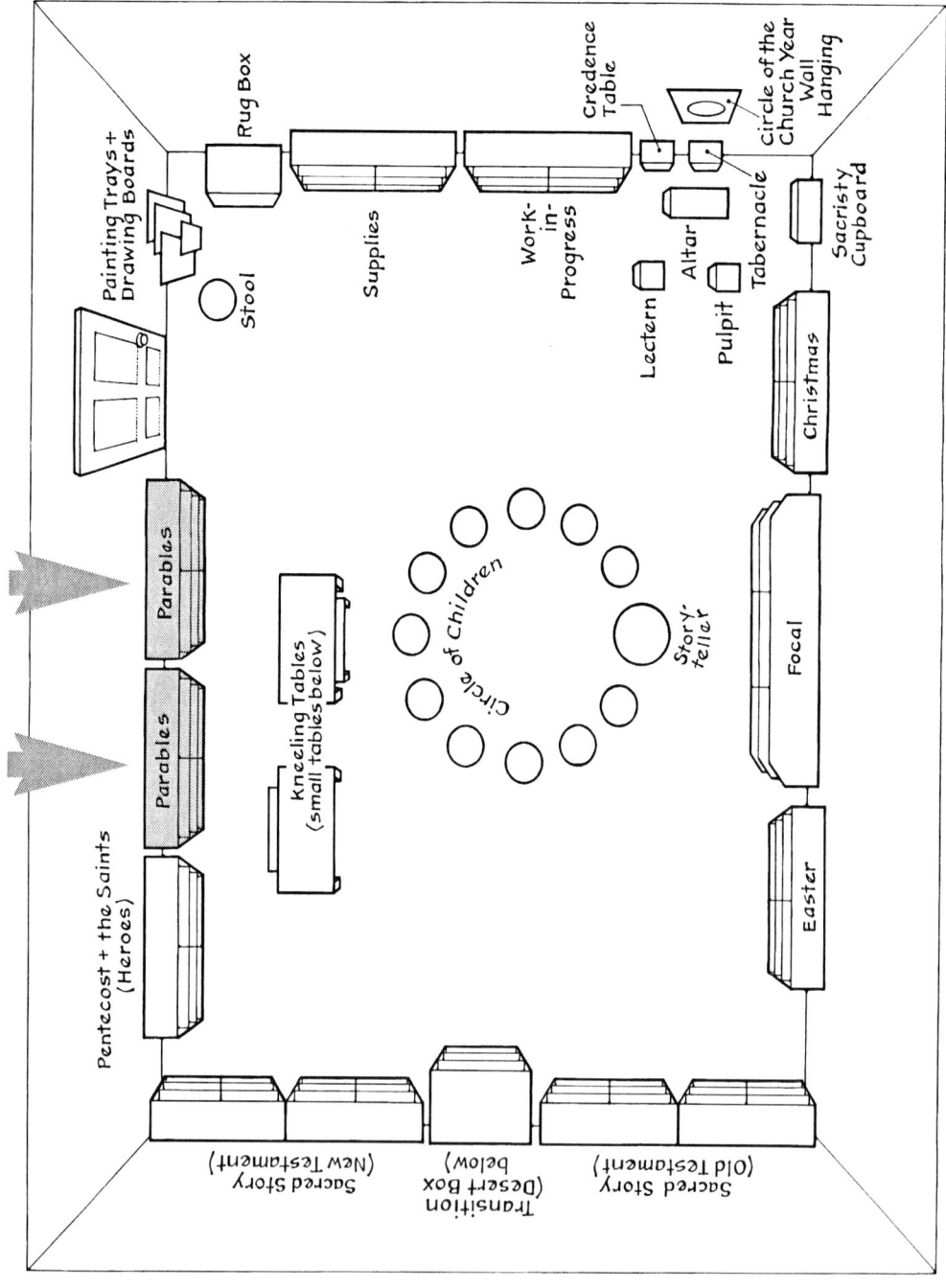

WHERE TO FIND MATERIALS

MOVEMENTS	WORDS
Go to the parable shelves and pick up the parable box. Point to the light brown dot on the box that identifies it. Bring the parable box to the circle of children.	Watch where I go to get this material.
Sit back and reflect for a moment about what might be inside. This is not a hypothetical exercise on the part of the storyteller. You have no guarantee that what you take out will be a parable. As you say to the children, parables can be easily broken when people are not ready. Even if you are ready, there are days when you will not find the presentation to be a parable.	Look, the box is the color gold. There may be a parable inside because parables are as valuable, or even more valuable, than gold. The box also looks like a present. Parables are presents. They were given to you before you were born. They are yours, even if you don't know what they are. This box looks old, and parables are old. Maybe there really is one inside. Do you see the lid? It is like a closed door. Sometimes parables seem closed to us, even if we are ready to enter them. You need to keep coming back for them, and one day they will open.
After using some or all these introductions, sit back a moment and reflect again on whether there is a parable inside the box. After a moment or two, you seem to have an idea.	I know what let's do. Let's look inside and see if there is a parable there.
Move the parable box from in front of you to your side. Remove the lid and lean it up against the box on the side where the children are sitting in the circle. This will help them keep focused on what is being presented rather than what is to come out of the box, and it helps keep the box more mysterious.	
Take out the underlay. Leave it in a crumpled heap in the middle of the circle. As you talk about it, begin to smooth it out.	I wonder what this could really be? It doesn't look like much now. Hmmm. It is certainly brown. It is all brown. Everywhere there is anything, there is brown. Let's see if there is anything else in the box that can help us get the parable ready.

Godly Play   *Parable of the Sower*

MOVEMENTS	WORDS
	There are many things here to help us tell the parable, but nothing else to help us get ready. All we can do then is begin.
	There was once someone who did such amazing things and said such wonderful things that people followed him. As they followed him, they heard him speaking about a kingdom. The kingdom was not like the one they were in. It was not like one that anyone had ever visited. It was not like any kingdom anyone had even heard about. So they had to ask him, "What is the kingdom of heaven like?"
Take the sower out of the box and place him on the underlay at your right facing toward the children.	One day when they asked him that, he said, "The kingdom of heaven is like when a sower, someone who scatters seeds, goes out and scatters seeds along the path."
Move the sower along the brown strip, scooping seeds from his basket with your hand, and sowing them along the underlay from your right to left. The sower stops.	
Take the gold box full of little birds from the parable box. Place it on the underlay between you and the "path." Remove the lid carefully.	"As the sower sowed seeds along the path, the birds of the air came..."
Take out the birds one by one and place them along the underlay (farthest from you) from your right to left. These are the birds who have come to eat the seeds.	"...and ate the seeds."
Take out the figure for the rocky ground and place it to your left of the birds that you lined up along the underlay farthest from you. Move the sower along that piece, scattering seeds from the bowl among the stones.	"The sower also sowed seeds among the stones."
The pushing down of the roots can be expressed with your hands by opening them and trying to push your fingers down among the stones.	"When the seeds tried to put their little roots down among the stones they could not push their way into the ground."
	"When the sun came out it scorched the seeds and they died."

Parable of the Sower

MOVEMENTS

Place the figure of the thorns to your left of the stones. Move the sower along the thorns, sowing as he goes.

The choking can be expressed by your hands. Clench both fists and twist them.

Place the figure of the good earth to your left of the thorns. Move the sower along the good earth and scatter seeds with your hand, scooping seeds from the bowl the sower carries.

Use your fingers again to show the roots going down into the earth.

Move your flat hand across the top of the figure showing the good earth, to show the cutting off of the ripe grain during the harvest.

Take out of the parable box the figures for the thirty, sixty and one hundred bushels and place them from your right to your left in ascending order along the underlay farthest away from you. "Fill them" by scooping up the harvest with your hand and "pouring" it into the containers, being sure the picture side is toward the children.

Pause for a moment after placing the containers of the harvest. Prepare yourself for the wondering. When you and the children are ready, begin.

Move the sower to the middle.

WORDS

"The sower also sowed seeds among the thorns."

"When the seeds tried to push their little roots down among the thorns, they could push them part way in, but the thorns choked them, and they died."

"The sower also sowed seeds in the good earth."

"When the seeds pushed their little roots down into the good earth, they could go all the way in. They grew and grew."

"When they were all grown up, they were ripe for the harvest. Then they were cut off and gathered up."

"The harvest was thirty, sixty and one hundred bushels."

Now, I wonder if the person had a name?

I wonder who the person could really be?

I wonder if the person was happy when the birds came and ate the seeds?

| **MOVEMENTS** | **WORDS** |

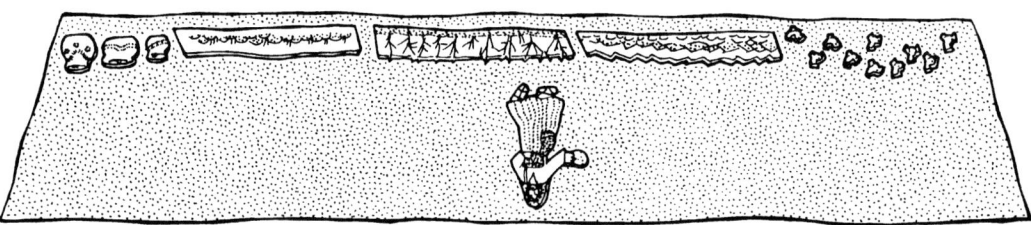

THE PARABLE OF THE SOWER (STORYTELLER'S PERSPECTIVE)

	I wonder if the birds were happy when they saw the sower?
	I wonder if the birds have names?
Move the sower from your right to left as you wonder.	I wonder what the person was doing when the little seeds could not get their roots in among the stones?
	I wonder what the person was doing when the little seeds were choked by the thorns?
	I wonder what the person was doing when the little seeds were growing in the good earth?
	I wonder what the harvest could really be?
Move the thorn figure above the stone figure and then put the good earth above the thorns. Then move the thirty bushels to the left of the stones, the sixty bushels to the left of the thorns, and the one hundred bushels to the left of the good earth.	Was it like this?
Put the thirty bushels by the good earth and the sixty by the stones and the one hundred by the thorns. Continue moving the harvest baskets until all possible combinations are completed.	Or could it really be like this?
Move everything back to its place. Then move the harvest bags to the middle between you and the soil strips. Touch each bag as you wonder how the harvest was used.	I wonder what the sower used for seed?
	I wonder what the sower sold?

MOVEMENTS

When the wondering winds down, begin to put all of the pieces of the parable carefully back in the parable box. Name the things as they are put away. Ask the children to begin thinking about what work they are going to get out during the response time.

When all is put away, replace the parable box on the shelf. Return to the circle of children and help them decide what work they would like to get out.

WORDS

I wonder what the sower kept for food?

I wonder if the sower was surprised at the harvest?

I wonder what part surprised the sower most?

Here are the birds.
Etc.

LITURGICAL LESSON
HOLY BAPTISM

LESSON NOTES
FOCUS: INITIATION BY WATER AND THE HOLY SPIRIT
- LITURGICAL ACTION
- CORE PRESENTATION

THE MATERIAL
- LOCATION: FOCAL SHELVES
- PIECES: LARGE TRAY HOLDING A BOWL (FOR THE BAPTISMAL FONT), PITCHER OF WATER, DOVE, CONTAINER OF FRAGRANT OIL, METAL BOX OF MATCHES, CANDLE SNUFFER AND WHITE UNDERLAYS; BASKET HOLDING A BABY DOLL, WRAPPED IN WHITE BLANKET OR GOWN; BRASS BOWL OF SAND; BASKET OF CANDLES, WITH DRIP GUARDS (OR CANDLES WITH HOLDERS); CHRIST CANDLE
- UNDERLAY: 3 WHITE FELT CIRCLES

BACKGROUND

You can present this lesson at any time during the Church year, but it is especially appropriate on the First Sunday after Epiphany (January 6), a Sunday known as the Baptism of Our Lord, or on any Sunday when a baptism is celebrated.

Holy Baptism is full initiation by water and the Holy Spirit into the Church. The rite draws both the past and future into the present, so there is no need to be baptized more than once. For Christians, this rite is the gateway into the family of families we call the Church. It remains the primary moment in the life of a Christian person to be remembered and looked forward to.

We baptize people in the traditional name of the Holy Trinity—Father, Son and Holy Spirit—so the primary material used in this lesson is three overlapping white circles, a well-known symbol of the Trinity. The names of Creator, Redeemer and Sustainer are juxtaposed to the classical language to show that the Trinity is about much more than gender.

We place images of action on each of the white circles: the pouring of water for the Creator, the lighting of the Christ Candle for the Redeemer, and the images of dove and the invisible scent of oil for the Sustainer. We ask children to remember or look forward to the day of their baptism by lighting candles from the light of the Christ Candle, since this is also the day they receive their "light."

NOTES ON THE MATERIAL

On a large tray place three rolled-up, white felt circles (each about 18" in diameter), a glass bowl (for the font, about 8" in diameter), a pitcher of water, a three-dimensional figure of a dove (about 5" in length), a small bottle or vial of fragrant oil, a metal box of matches and a candle snuffer. In a basket you need to have a baby doll, wrapped in a white blanket or dressed in a white gown. You also need a brass bowl (about 8" in diameter) half filled with sand and a second basket holding small candles (about ½" in diameter and 4" tall) fitted with drip guards, to protect the children's hands from hot wax. For children too small to handle candles, provide candles (tapers or votives) in holders, one to place in front of each child. You will also need the Christ Candle.

Find the materials for this presentation on the focal shelves. The Christ Candle sits on the top focal shelf, to the left. The tray of materials and basket with the doll are on the middle focal shelf, directly underneath the Christ Candle (to the left). The basket of small candles and bowl of sand are on the bottom focal shelf, underneath the other baptism materials (to the left).

Adapt the materials according to the usage of your church. For example, if your church uses a shell for baptism, you can place one on the tray with the other materials. If your tradition baptizes by total immersion, you will need to work out a way to show that, perhaps using a larger bowl or basin as the font instead of the bowl described above.

SPECIAL NOTES

Classroom Management: When the lesson about Holy Baptism is presented to the children, it is not a baptism, nor is it playing at baptism. Instead, the lesson invites children to "remember the day of their baptism or look forward to the day of their baptism." Thus we use a doll rather than a real person.

Cleaning supplies for the children to use should include polishing materials. Children will enjoy polishing the metal parts of the materials used in today's presentation. Some children will want to choose polishing for their individual work.

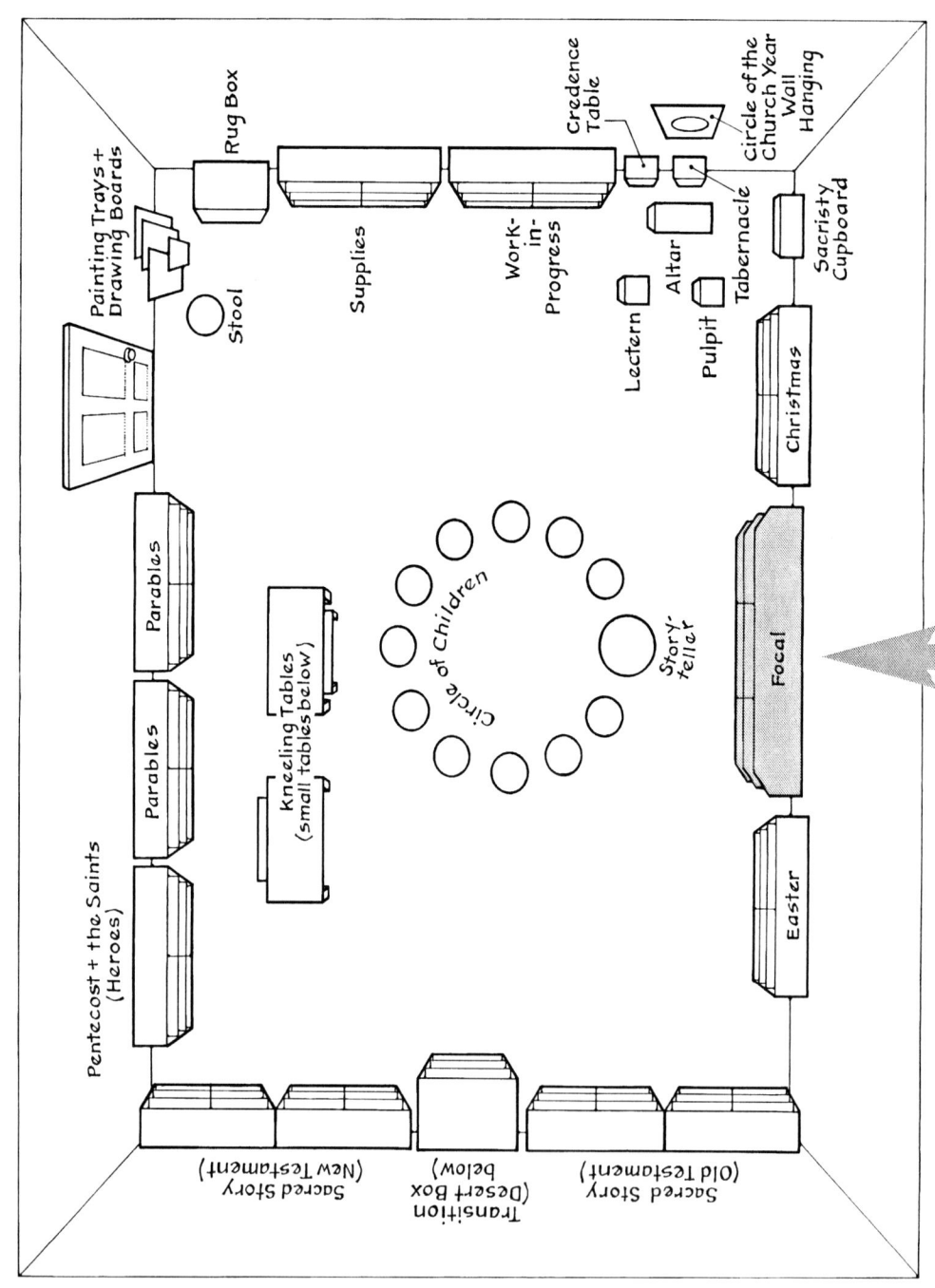

WHERE TO FIND MATERIALS

MOVEMENTS

Before the lesson, fill the pitcher with water and check the matches. Will they strike?

When the children are settled, get up and walk around the room. Then come back to where you were seated, in front of the focal shelves.

The Baptism materials are on the lower focal shelves, beneath the Christ Candle, which is on the left of the top focal shelf.

Bring to the circle the large tray, the two baskets and the bowl with sand in it. Place these on either side of where you will be sitting.

Get the Christ Candle. When you are settled and when the children are ready, begin.

Unroll the first white circle. Smooth it out. Unroll the second circle and place it so that it smoothly overlaps the first. Unroll the third one and place it so that it smoothly overlaps the first two circles.

Sit back and appreciate this symbol of the Trinity. Then point to each circle and name them again.

Place the pitcher and the glass bowl on the Father circle, the Christ Candle on the Son circle, and the dove and oil on the Holy Spirit circle. Do this slowly and with deliberation.

WORDS

Watch. Watch where I go to get this lesson. Here are the Sacred Stories. Here are the parables. Here are liturgical action lessons.

Oh. This is the lesson about Baptism.

We need something else.

We baptize people in the name of the Father...the Son...and the Holy Spirit.

The Creator, the Redeemer, the Sustainer.

MOVEMENTS

WORDS

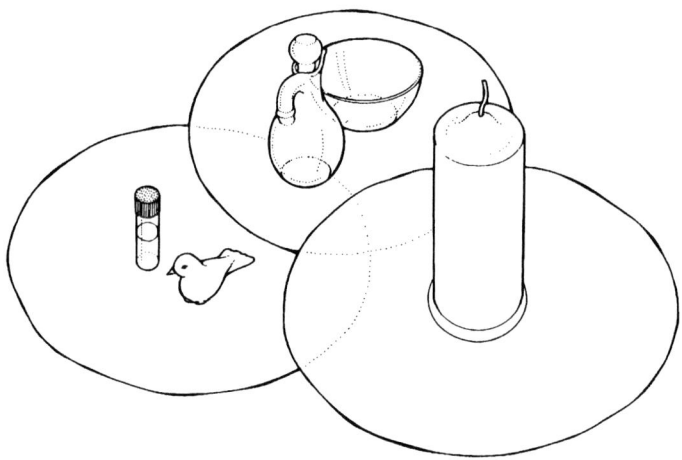

THE THREE CIRCLES OF THE TRINITY (STORYTELLER'S PERSPECTIVE)

Pour the water into the glass bowl, listening to the sound of the water. Then put your hand in the water and move it as you begin to name it. Then cup your hand to draw out some water and pour it back as you continue.	This is the water of creation, the dangerous water of the flood, the water the people went through into freedom, the water Jesus was baptized in, the water you were—or will be—baptized in, and so much more.
When you have contemplated this for a moment, take a match from its container and point to the Christ Candle.	There was once someone who said such wonderful things and did such amazing things that people just had to ask him who he was. One time when they asked him who he was, he said…
Strike the match and light the Christ Candle.	"…I am the Light."
Take the stopper from the container of oil. Move the container slowly around the circle so children can catch its fragrance.	The Holy Spirit goes where it will. It rides the invisible wind like a dove and comes to us when we need its comfort and power. It is invisible, like the scent of this oil. It is invisible but still there.
	People are baptized when they are babies, or children, or teenagers, or grownups, or when they are very old. We will use a baby doll to see how this is done.
Pick up the doll and hold it in your arms.	We ask the person about to be baptized questions, or if it's a baby too little to answer, we ask the parents or godparents. We say prayers for them. Then we are ready.

68   *Holy Baptism*   *Godly Play*

MOVEMENTS

WORDS

But wait. What is the name of this child? Names are very important in baptism.

Take the first name you get and quickly move on.

"Bobby." That's a good name.

Stir the water and put it on the doll's head, or pour some on, or immerse the doll.

Bobby, I baptize you in the name of the Father...and of the Son...and of the Holy Spirit. Amen.

Put some of the oil on your fingers or thumb and make the sign of the cross on the doll's forehead, if that is your church's custom.

Bobby, you are sealed by the Holy Spirit in baptism and marked as Christ's own forever. Amen.

Carefully place the doll back in its basket. Then, pick up a candle from the candle basket.

This is the day when Bobby receives her light. We light it from the Christ Candle.

Name this child.

When you or the children respond, "Bobby," continue.

Bobby, remember the day of your baptism.

Light Bobby's candle and place it in the bowl of sand. Pick up another candle from the candle basket to use for yourself.

Name this child. *(Say your own name.)* Remember the day of your baptism.

Place your candle in the bowl of sand. Pass the basket of candles so each child can have one. Repeat the naming and candle-lighting ritual for each child. The children can hold the lit candles, or, if they are not ready for this responsibility, can place them in the bowl of sand.

As the candles are being lit, call the children's attention to the expanding circle of light.

Look. The light is growing bigger and bigger. Look here. The light that all the light is coming from is not growing smaller. I wonder how so much light can come from one light?

See. Look at all this light.

MOVEMENTS

Pick up the candle snuffer.

Slowly place the candle snuffer over the flame. Hold it down until the flame is out. Raise the candle snuffer slowly and allow the smoke to rise and expand into the room.

The children take turns changing their light. Then pass the candle basket again so the children can place the extinguished candles in it. Finally, change the light of the Christ Candle.

Some children may not want to change their lights. They can leave them lit by placing them in the sand of the bowl (if they have not already done so). During the session, the candles will melt down and form a single candle with several wicks still flickering with light.

You can omit the wondering after this lesson. The lesson itself holds enormous wonder, and it is somewhat long. Put everything carefully back on the tray and in the baskets. Return the materials to the appropriate shelves. Carry the bowl of sand to the top shelf beside the Christ Candle if there are candles still burning in it. Otherwise, you can replace it on the lowest shelf.

Often there will be no time for a work period after this lesson, so you may proceed directly to the feast.

WORDS

Now let me show you something. Let's change the light. No. I did not say we were going to put it out or extinguish it. Watch. I will show you with mine first.

Do you see how all the light is right here in the flame? It is easy to see then. Now watch. It changes.

See? The light is still spreading out. It is filling up the room. Just because you can't see it anymore doesn't mean that it is gone. Anywhere you go in the room today, there it will be. Our room will be full of invisible light. Your light. The light you received on the day of your Baptism or the light you will receive.

If you don't want to change your light, you may come forward very carefully and put your candle in the sand.

LITURGICAL LESSON
THE GOOD SHEPHERD AND WORLD COMMUNION

LESSON NOTES

FOCUS: THE GOOD SHEPHERD AND HOLY COMMUNION

- LITURGICAL ACTION
- CORE PRESENTATION

THE MATERIAL

- LOCATION: FOCAL SHELVES
- PIECES: GOOD SHEPHERD, SHEEP, SHEEPFOLD, TABLE, PRIEST, PEOPLE OF THE WORLD, SMALL CONTAINER HOLDING A PATEN AND CHALICE
- UNDERLAY: 2 CIRCLES COVERED IN GREEN FELT

BACKGROUND

The images of the Good Shepherd and Holy Communion deepen each other's interpretation when set side by side like this. One does not need to step outside the domain of religious language into the language of philosophy or science, for example, to talk *about* the two religious images or interpret them. One can remain *within* religious language, meditating, while the images disclose the depths in each other.

For older children, you can also place other presentations side by side. For example, lay out the story of the Exodus (pp. 65-72, *The Complete Guide to Godly Play, Volume 2*) next to this story. Ask, "I wonder what in *this* story (the Exodus) belongs in *this* story (the Good Shepherd and World Communion)?" and *vice versa*.

Note: This lesson was suggested by the work of Sofia Cavalletti. The reader should be aware, however, that both the teaching material and the lesson are substantially changed and put to a different use in Godly Play than in her work. Please see *The Complete Guide to Godly Play, Volume 1*, Chapter 6, pp. 86-107, "Entering the Tradition," for further information.

NOTES ON THE MATERIAL

In an ideal setup, the focal shelves are the shelf unit directly opposite the door that the children enter. The Holy Family sits in the center of the top shelf. To the right of the Holy Family as you face the shelves is one green circle with the figure of the Good Shepherd, the sheepfold and his sheep. (The sheepfold is a set of hinged wooden fence pieces.) On the shelf below the Good Shepherd and his sheep, there is another green circle with a table standing at its center. On the shelf below the second circle, there is a basket that holds a priest, the people of the world and a small container. The container holds a paten and chalice to represent the bread and wine.

SPECIAL NOTES

As you can see, this is a core presentation for the liturgical action part of the Christian tradition of communion, as conceived of in Godly Play. It is not included among the parable lessons, because parables function in a different way than liturgical action, although there is always some overlap. This presentation does tell a story, but it is not part of the sacred story materials because it focuses on the liturgical action and the symbols by which that action carries its meaning to us and to which we respond.

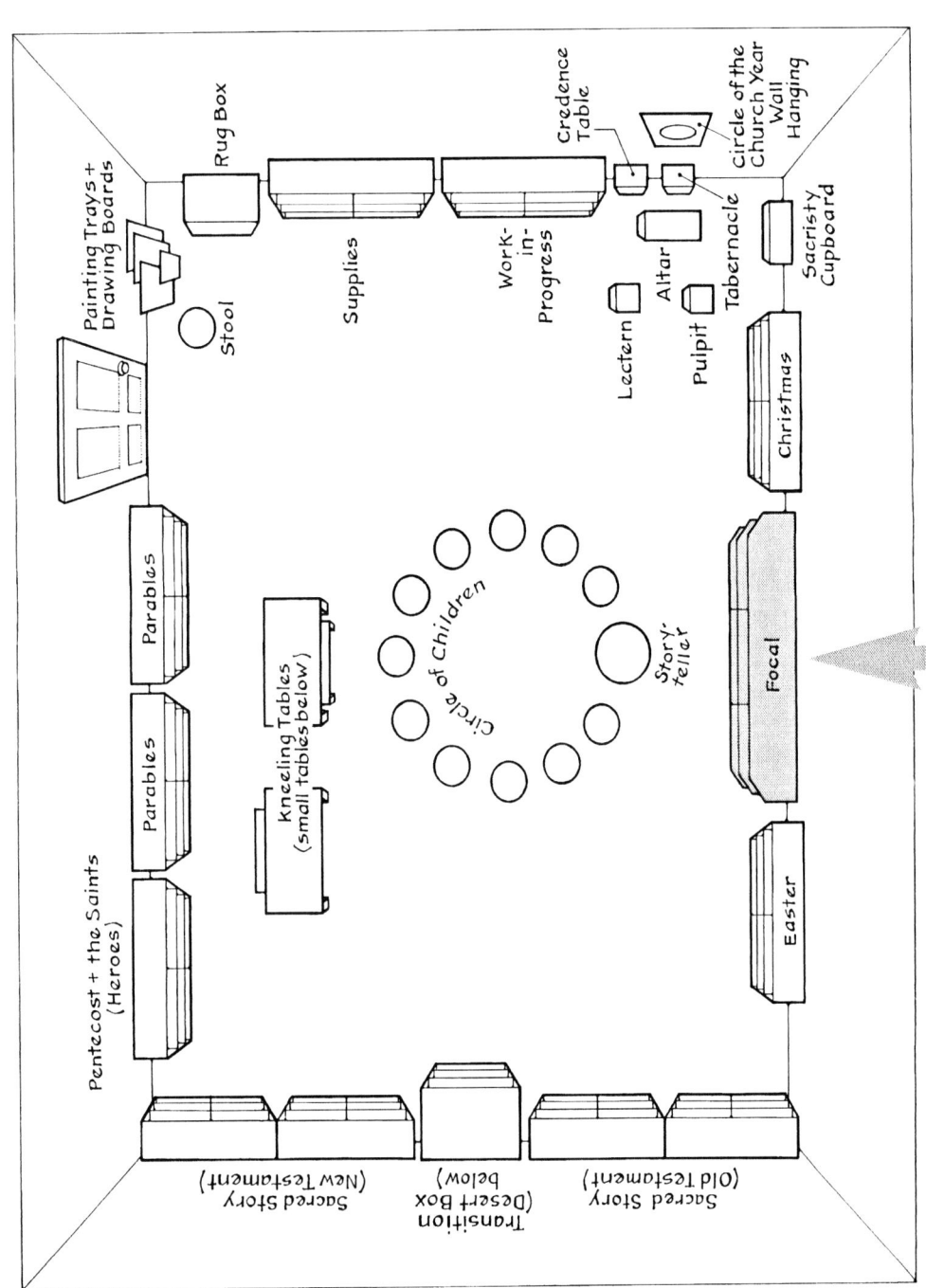

WHERE TO FIND MATERIALS

Godly Play   *The Good Shepherd and World Communion*   73

MOVEMENTS

Even though the material is right behind you, on the focal shelves, get up and walk around the circle to find the material. This is much more dramatic than merely reaching out to pull the pieces off the shelves. The children will gain a better sense of where the material is.

Carry the material carefully, with two hands, as you want the children to carry it. First bring the green circle with the Good Shepherd, the sheepfold and the sheep to the storytelling circle. Place it in front of where you will be sitting. Then return to the shelf for the second circle with the table on it.

Bring the second green circle to the storytelling circle. Then return to the shelves and bring the basket with the people of the world and the small container.

Put the two green circles next to each other, touching. The one on the right in front of you, the storyteller, is the Good Shepherd, and the one on your left is the Table. Put the basket to the right and a little behind where you are sitting. The point is to get this out of the way, so it will not distract the children until you are ready to use it.

The sheepfold, sheep and shepherd are arranged as shown here.

WORDS

Watch carefully where I go so you will know where to find this material. Watch with your eyes.

You see, there is a lot to bring. This is big work. Watch carefully.

THE SHEPHERD AND THE SHEEPFOLD (STORYTELLER'S PERSPECTIVE)

MOVEMENTS	WORDS
Sit for a brief time to let the children settle. If they have trouble getting ready, work with them until they are settled. Then begin.	There was once someone who did such wonderful things and said such amazing things that people wondered who he was. Finally they just couldn't help it. They had to ask him who he was.
Touch the head of the Good Shepherd figure.	When they asked him who he was, he said, "I am the Good Shepherd."
Run your thumb down the back of the neck of each sheep.	"I know each one of the sheep by name, and they know the sound of my voice."
Move the Good Shepherd out of the sheepfold and around to your right. Move him halfway around to a position at the bottom of the circle in front of you. Then go back and move each one of the sheep to catch up with him. They stay in single file. Keep silence while you are doing this and just enjoy watching the sheep.	"When I take the sheep from the sheepfold, they follow me."

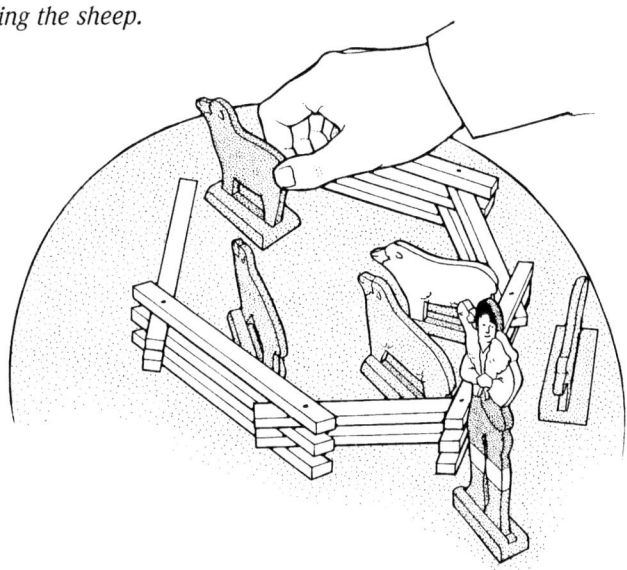

OUTSIDE THE SHEEPFOLD (STORYTELLER'S PERSPECTIVE)

Move the Good Shepherd from the bottom position on the right circle to the top position on the left circle. Take your time.	"I walk in front of the sheep to show them the way."

Godly Play   The Good Shepherd and World Communion

MOVEMENTS

WORDS

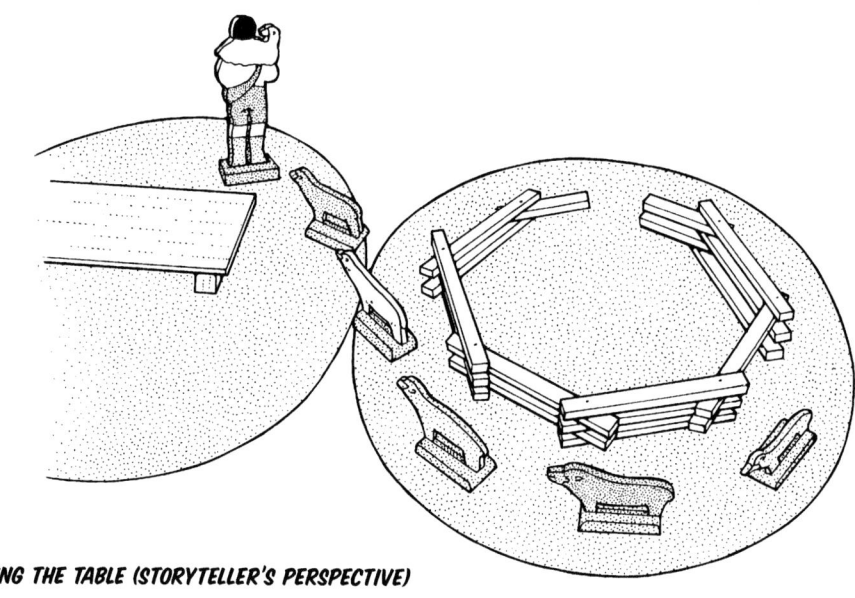

APPROACHING THE TABLE (STORYTELLER'S PERSPECTIVE)

Move the sheep up to where the Good Shepherd is. Move them one at a time. Think about what is happening as you move them from one circle to the other.

"I show them the way to the good grass."

Without saying anything else, move the Good Shepherd to the bottom position of the left-hand circle and move the sheep so that they are spread out equally now around the table but still turned as if they are following around the edge of the circle.

When all of the sheep are in position, move the Good Shepherd forward to stand behind the table (from the child's perspective). Turn all of the sheep so they are facing the table.

MOVEMENTS

WORDS

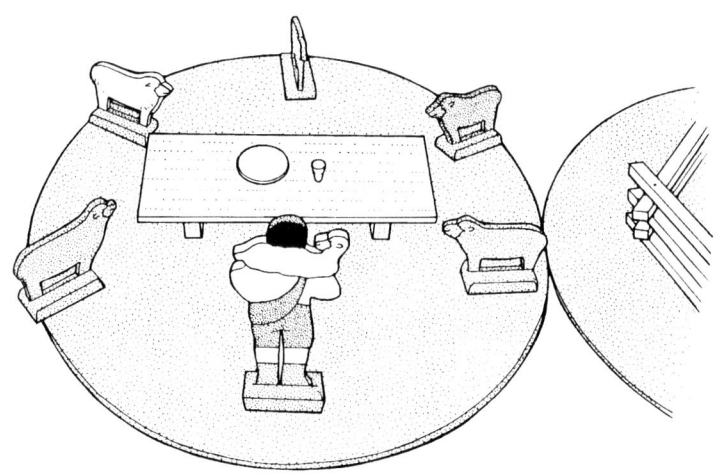

AROUND THE TABLE (STORYTELLER'S PERSPECTIVE)

Trace the outside rim of the table.	This is the table of the Good Shepherd.
Get the chalice and paten from the basket and place them on the table.	Here is the bread and wine of the Good Shepherd. Sometimes it seems like we need to have a little statue or something on the table to remind us that this is the table of the Good Shepherd, but the Good Shepherd is in the bread and the wine, so we don't really need anything to remind us.
Remove the Good Shepherd. Bring out the priest and move the priest into the position behind the table where the Good Shepherd was.	Sometimes someone comes to read the very words of the Good Shepherd, and to give us the bread and the wine.
Take one of the adult human figures from the basket. Show it to the children, then put it between the sheep. Continue doing this until all the adults from around the world are in place.	Sometimes the people of the world come to this table, and...
Take out the child figures and put them by the adult figures. Do not group the figures by gender, ethnicity or culture. The world no longer works like that.	...even the children come.

Godly Play — The Good Shepherd and World Communion

MOVEMENTS

WORDS

THE PEOPLE AROUND THE TABLE (STORYTELLER'S PERSPECTIVE)

Sit and look at the people of the world around the table for a moment, then begin the wondering.	Now I wonder if you have ever come close to this table?
	I wonder where this table could really be?
Trace the outline of the table with your finger. Don't hurry the children. Give them time to wonder.	I wonder if the people are happy around this table?
	I wonder if you have ever heard the words of the Good Shepherd?
	I wonder if you have ever come close to the bread and the wine?
	I wonder where the bread and the wine could really be?
Move your hand over both circles.	I wonder where this whole place could really be?
When the wondering draws to a close, turn the children's attention toward getting out their own work.	

LITURGICAL LESSON
THE CIRCLE OF THE CHURCH YEAR

LESSON NOTES
FOCUS: HOW THE CHURCH TELLS TIME
- LITURGICAL ACTION
- CORE PRESENTATION

THE MATERIAL
- LOCATION: FOCAL SHELVES
- PIECES: CIRCLE OF THE CHURCH YEAR WALL HANGING, CIRCLE OF THE CHURCH YEAR PRESENTATION SET
- UNDERLAY: USE A SOLID-COLORED RUG

BACKGROUND

This lesson sets the context for the whole year. Each year, the Christian people move through a circle of memory and expectation to open themselves to the elusive presence of God. In the Godly Play classroom, we pay attention to this circle of movement each week.

This lesson uses the Circle of the Church Year presentation set (illustrated on p. 27), which includes a circular frame, fifty-two removable colored blocks and a gold cord or ribbon.

You'll also use the Circle of the Church Year wall hanging (illustrated on p. 24), which has colored cloth "blocks" for the Sundays of the year and a golden arrow that moves from Sunday to Sunday. From now on, begin each class by inviting a child to go to this wall hanging and move the golden arrow to the next Sunday. (Check the wall hanging before class to make sure that when the child moves the arrow to the next block, it will point to the right color.) This invites children to move through the Church's special kind of time, marked not by numbers but by blocks of color.

NOTES ON THE MATERIAL

The Circle of the Church Year presentation set is a circle about one foot in diameter made from wood, poster board, foamcore or felt. Blocks made from the same material fit in a ring to mark each week of the liturgical year, as well as the day of Christmas.

Three arrow-shaped hands of this "clock" point to the three great times of the Church year. If you buy only one ready-made material, we recommend that it be this one. Accurately cutting out these blocks is a difficult job!

This material can either be kept inside a box or set plainly on the shelf. A box adds to the mystery; without a box, children can see the material better when they look around the room. Some sets, intended for older children, include inserts that fit inside the circle. These inserts are labeled with the names of the seasons, months, phases of the moon, etc., so a child can actually find the date of Easter for any given year.

You will use the gold cord or ribbon (about three feet long) to show how time can be "in a line." this cord needs to be flexible and small enough to curl up inside your fist.

Traditions about the use of color for feast days or liturgical seasons vary greatly, even within denominations. As you order the material or prepare this lesson, please adjust as needed to match the colors actually used in your church.

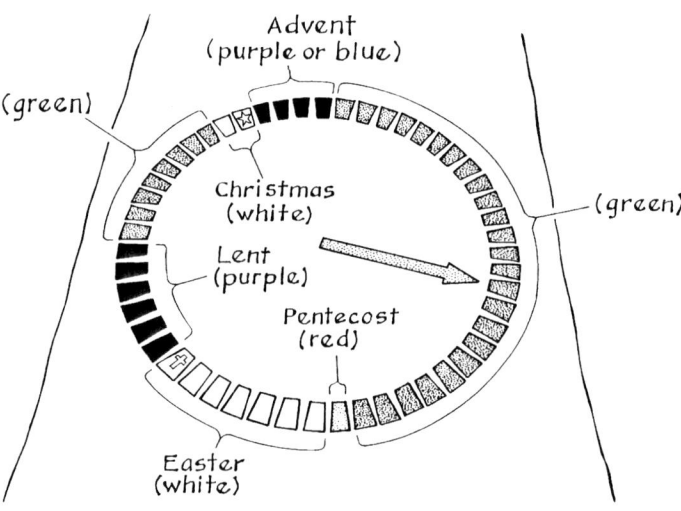

CIRCLE OF THE CHURCH YEAR WALL HANGING

SPECIAL NOTES

Art Project: Although we rarely suggest specific art projects, children might enjoy making their own Circle of the Church Year to take home. Cut out two circles to match the inside and outside diameters of the presentation material's circular slot. The children use these to trace their own circles. They then glue "blocks" made from construction paper between the two lines, using the wall hanging or presentation material for their guide. Finally, they attach the golden arrow to the center of the circle. The individual precut, colored blocks and the arrows and brads for attaching them are kept in their own clear plastic containers. All materials are kept together on a tray. Invite children to take their completed circles with them, so they can follow the Circle of the Church Year at home, the way they do in class.

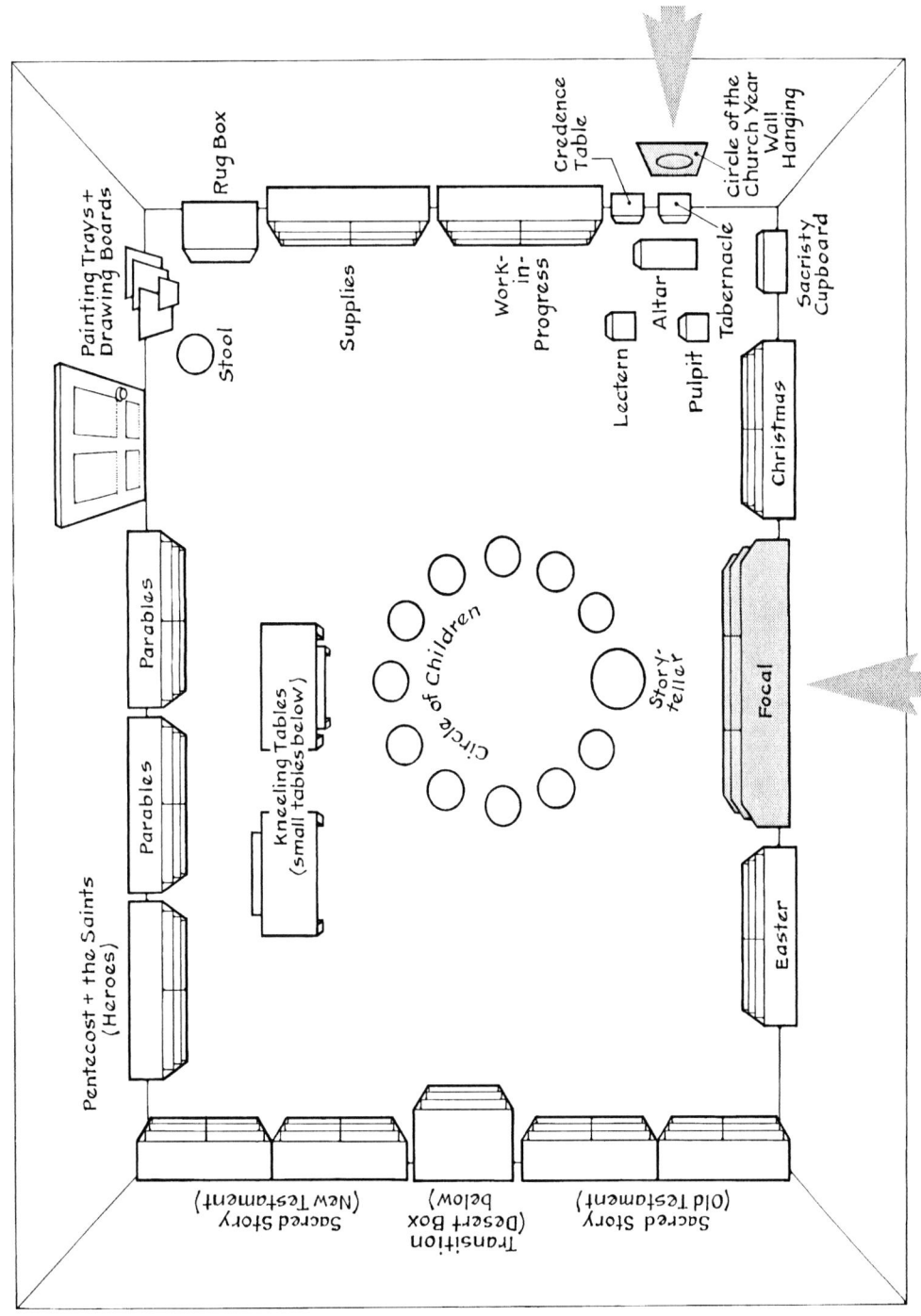

WHERE TO FIND MATERIALS

MOVEMENTS	**WORDS**
Get up from your position in the circle and carefully cross the room to the rug box. Pick up a rug with attentive care.	Now watch carefully. Here is the rug you need for this lesson.
Bring the rug to the circle and roll it out just as carefully and lovingly as you would like the children to do. This is especially important for children younger than eight years old.	Watch where I go now to get the lesson.
The Circle of the Church Year material is usually kept right behind the story teller, so why walk around the room? Reaching back and pulling it off the shelf isn't dramatic enough to catch the children's attention and help them remember where to find the story. Instead, get up and walk around the room until you come back to where the circle sits on its shelf.	Hm. It's not where the sacred stories are. It's not where the parables are. Ah, here it is! This is the lesson about the Circle of the Church Year.
Sit down in the circle with the rug in front of you. Place the material to your side. As you do so, pick up the gold cord and enclose it in your hand so that you can pull it out through a space between two fingers. Keep eye contact with the children as you hide the cord in your hand and begin the story.	
	Time, time, time. There are all kinds of time. There is a time to get up in the morning. There is a time to go to bed. There is a time to go to school and a time to come home. There is a time to work, and there is a time to play. But what is time?
Until now, the gold cord has been hidden. But now you show a small end of the cord extending between your fingers, and you suddenly notice it.	Some people say that time is in a line, but I wonder what that would look like? Ah. Wait a minute. What is this?

MOVEMENTS	**WORDS**
	Time. Time in a line. This is time in a line. Look at this. Here is the beginning. It is the newest part. It is just being born. It is brand new. Now look.
Pull out the cord slowly as you speak. Pull it all the way out from your fist slowly as you talk until it drops to the rug.	Look. It is getting older. The part that was new is now getting old. I wonder how long time goes. Does it go forever? Could there ever be an ending?
The end of the cord drops.	It ended. Look at the ending.
Pick up the cord and look at it.	
Hold the two ends and look at them.	The beginning that was so new at the beginning now is old. The ending is the new part now. We have a beginning that is like an ending and an ending that is like a beginning.
Tie the two ends (beginnings) together. Then put the circle of wooden blocks on the rug and place the golden circle of time around the circle of the material.	Do you know what the Church did? They tied the ending that was like a beginning, and the beginning that was like an ending together, so we would always remember that for every ending there is a beginning and for every beginning there is an ending.

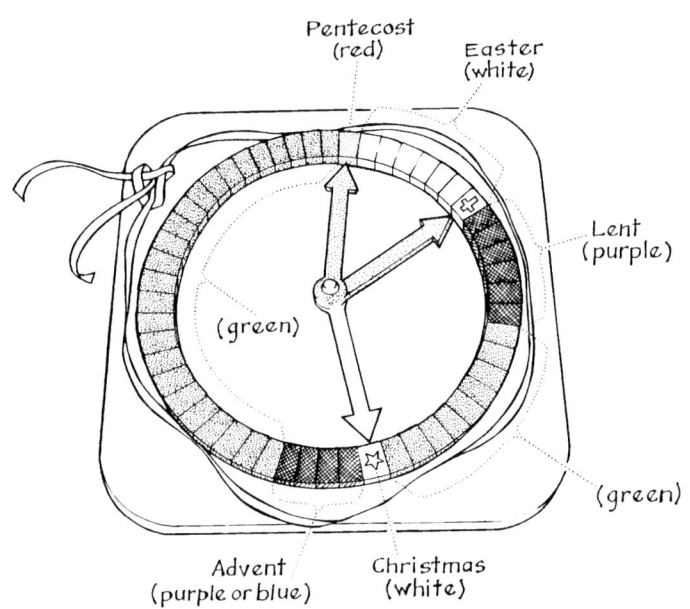

CIRCLE OF THE CHURCH YEAR PRESENTATION SET (STORYTELLER'S PERSPECTIVE)

MOVEMENTS	**WORDS**
Leave the golden cord on the material and begin to remove the blocks. Begin with the "three great times" (a white Christmas block, a white Easter block and a red Pentecost block). When you pick up the red Pentecost block, drop it briefly: it's so hot! Remember to speak of the three great "times," since Christmas is not always on a Sunday.	Here are the three great times. This is Christmas. This is Easter. This is—ouch! That's hot! This is Pentecost.
Sit back for a moment and look at the blocks for the three great times.	People can walk right through these mysteries each year, and not even know what's there. We need time to get ready to come close to these mysteries.
Place the four purple (or blue) blocks of Advent in a line to your right of the white block for Christmas. Place the six purple blocks for Lent in a line to your right of the white block for Easter.	Here are the times for getting ready. The time for getting ready to come close to the mystery of Christmas is called "Advent." The time for getting ready to come close to the mystery of Easter is called "Lent."
Touch first the four blocks of Advent, then the six blocks of Lent.	Look. The time for getting ready to come close to the mystery of Easter is longer than the time for getting ready to come close to the mystery of Christmas. This is because Easter is an even greater mystery than Christmas.
Count out six more white Sunday blocks for the season of Easter and place them to your right of the red block for Pentecost.	It is so great that it keeps on going. You can't keep it in one Sunday. It overflows and goes on for six more Sundays. It makes a whole season!
Touch Pentecost again, but snatch your hand away because it's still hot.	The season of Easter is also a time for getting ready to come close to the mystery of Pentecost. Ouch! It's still hot.
Now only green blocks are left in the circle. Begin to remove them in groups of three, and place them on the rug in groups of three. Refer to the diagram for correct placement. Pace yourself: you don't want to rush, but you do want to get the blocks out before the children lose interest.	Here are all of the great, green Sundays of the year.

MOVEMENTS

WORDS

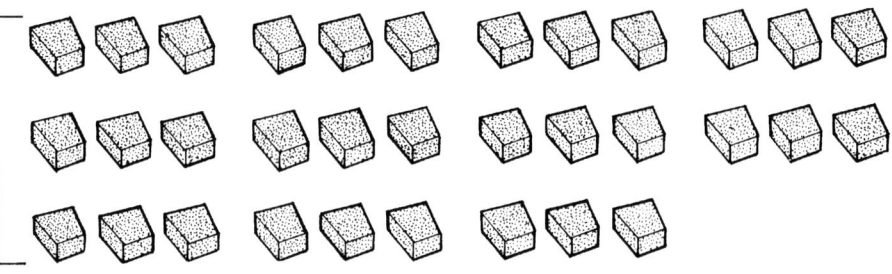

Great, Green, Growing Sundays (green)

Pentecost (red) — Easter (white)

Easter (white) — Lent (purple)

Christmas (white) — Advent (purple or blue)

ALL THE BLOCKS OUT OF THE CIRCLE (STORYTELLER'S PERSPECTIVE)

Now let's see if we can build the circle of the year again. Watch carefully, because the Church tells time by colors as well as by clocks.

Place the white block for Christmas in the empty circle, then the white Easter block and finally the red Pentecost block.

Here are the three great times.

Ouch, it's still hot.

Put the blocks in their approximate final spaces but slide them around to show that those places are not yet set.

Godly Play   *The Circle of the Church Year*   85

MOVEMENTS	WORDS

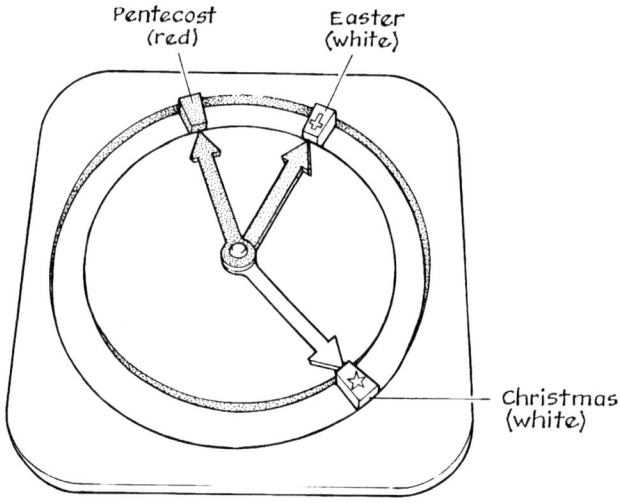

THE THREE GREAT TIMES IN THE CIRCLE (STORYTELLER'S PERSPECTIVE)

Place the four purple (or blue) blocks for Advent in front of the white Christmas block. Touch each block in turn as you count one, two, three, four.	The time for getting ready for the mystery of Christmas is called Advent. It is one, two, three, four weeks long. The Church year begins with the beginning of Advent.
	Sometimes the color for getting ready for Christmas is purple. That's a serious color, the color of kings. Sometimes the color is blue. Do you know why? Because it's one of the colors for the Mother Mary. Without the Mother Mary, there would be no baby Jesus.
Place the six purple blocks for Lent in front of the white Easter block.	The time for getting ready for Easter is usually purple. Purple is the color of kings, and something is going to happen to Jesus, the King. But he was not the kind of king that people thought was coming. He was a different kind of king.
Touch each of the purple Lent blocks in turn as you count one, two, three, four, five, six.	Look, there are one, two, three, four, five, six weeks for getting ready for Easter. It is an even greater mystery than Christmas, so it takes longer to get ready to enter it.
Place the six white blocks for the season of Easter after the block for Easter itself. Touch each block as you count one, two, three, four, five, six.	Easter is so great a mystery that you can't keep it in only one Sunday. It keeps on going for one, two, three, four, five, six weeks.
	During that time people met Jesus in a new way. He had died on the cross, and that was very sad. But they kept meeting him.

MOVEMENTS	**WORDS**
	Somehow Jesus was still with them, as he is still with us.
	Then something wonderful happened. The Apostles went outside of Jerusalem with Jesus in this new way.
Put your two hands over the circle like a blessing. Raise them together about 12".	There they saw him go up.
Move one hand back down and touch the Pentecost block.	And a few days later the Holy Spirit came down. The Church was born. The Apostles glowed with the power of the Holy Spirit. Their tongues were like fire when they spoke. They were more alive than they had ever been before. That's why the color of Pentecost is red like fire.
Begin to put the green blocks into the circle, three at a time. First place nine green blocks between the white Christmas block and the first purple block of Lent.	First we will put in the great, green, growing Sundays between Christmas and the beginning of Lent. The most you can ever have here are nine, so we will put in nine green growing weeks here.
Next place the remaining green blocks, three at a time, between the red Pentecost block and the first purple block of Advent. Take your time and let the children's year unfold in their imaginations as you replace these great, green Sundays.	Here are the rest of the great, green, growing Sundays. Do you know what the Sundays after Pentecost are called? They are called "the Sundays after Pentecost."
	Here is the time when school is out. The summer comes and the days get longer and longer. You can play outside later. People go swimming. Some go to camp. Many go on vacation. Then summer comes to an end.
	Now you begin to get ready for school. You need new clothes and books. School begins and you often have a new teacher. The days get shorter. School goes on and you get used to all the new things.
	Now the days are really short. It gets dark very early. It looks as if the light is just about to go out. Right at that time, when the light seems to be coming to an end, we reach Advent. The year ends, and it begins again. It is time to get ready to enter the mystery of Christmas.

MOVEMENTS	WORDS

These can be shown by the "clock hands" that extend from the middle of the circle to the Christmas, Easter and Pentecost blocks.

Here are the three great times: Christmas. Easter. Pentecost.

If you have inserts that fit inside the circle to label the seasons, you can name the seasons once again as you put the inserts in. These pieces should be cut to the exact length of each area's name, so that older children can check their own work when using this material. If you don't have these inserts, simply touch the blocks named.

Here are the times for getting ready. Advent. That's four weeks. Lent. That's six weeks. You can't keep Easter to just one Sunday, so it keeps on for six more weeks. Those weeks are called the season of Easter, too. Here are the great, green, growing Sundays of the year.

Move your hand around the reassembled circle.

It is all here. Everything we need. For every beginning there is an ending, and for every ending there is a beginning. It goes on and on, forever and ever.

Sit back and enjoy the whole circle of beautiful colors. Now it's time to begin the wondering.

I wonder which one of these colors you like best?

I wonder how the colors make you feel?

I wonder which color is the most important?

These last wondering questions are especially intended to prepare children for a visit to the sacristy, with its mysterious cupboards and wonderful drawers of colors. If possible, arrange for such a visit in the next week or so.

I wonder if you have ever seen these colors in the church?

Some of the colors in the church change, and some do not. I wonder where the ones are that change?

I wonder if you have ever come close to these colors in the church?

I wonder what happens in the church when you see these colors?

I wonder who changes the colors there?

I wonder where the colors go when you do not see them?

I wonder why the Church tells time with colors?

MOVEMENTS

Model how you want the children to put the materials away by walking carefully around the circle, carrying the materials with two hands. Return them to the shelf. Then carefully roll up the rug and return it to the rug box.

Begin helping the children decide on their responses. Today you can include the possibility of children making their own circles to take home. See the Special Notes (p. 24) for details.

You might also have a page from a calendar mounted on foamcore to lay beside the circle when you wonder why the Church tells time with colors.

WORDS

Now watch carefully where I go to put this lesson away, so you will always know where to find it.

LITURGICAL LESSON
THE MYSTERY OF EASTER

FOCUS: LENT, THE MYSTERY OF EASTER AND THE EASTER SEASON
- LITURGICAL ACTION
- CORE PRESENTATION

THE MATERIAL
- LOCATION: EASTER SHELVES
- PIECES: PURPLE AND WHITE BAG, SIX PUZZLE PIECES
- UNDERLAY: NONE

BACKGROUND

Lent is the season when we prepare for Easter. These six weeks are a solemn time, overflowing with meaning, when we view life from the perspective of our existential limits and the sacrifice of Christ. This lesson gives an introduction to the relationship of Lent to the Mystery of Easter as well as how Easter overflows into the *season* of Easter. Follow this introduction by presenting the lessons of the Faces of Easter during the weeks of Lent.

NOTES ON THE MATERIAL

Find the materials for this presentation on the top shelf of the Easter shelves. To the right will be the material for the Faces of Easter.

A bag, which is purple on the outside and white on the inside, holds six puzzle pieces, which, when assembled, make the shape of the cross. One side of the cross is purple; the other side of the cross is white. It is much more than a puzzle with pieces that fit together, as you will see from how the lesson ends in the Mystery and season of Easter.

SPECIAL NOTES

Storytelling Tip: Remember that this story is called the Mystery of *Easter*, not the Mystery of Lent. The fullest meaning of Lent is that it gives us time to prepare for the great Mystery of Easter, the principal feast of the Christian Church. Similarly, we recommend that you not call the material a "cross puzzle" but always refer to it as "the material for the Mystery of Easter."

On the First Sunday of Lent, we recommend that you first focus on the change of seasons. Use the Holy Family presentation to change the focal shelf color from green to purple. Then tell the Mystery of Easter. Most often, that will be all the material suitable for the First Sunday of Lent. You can combine two of the Faces presentations on the next Sunday.

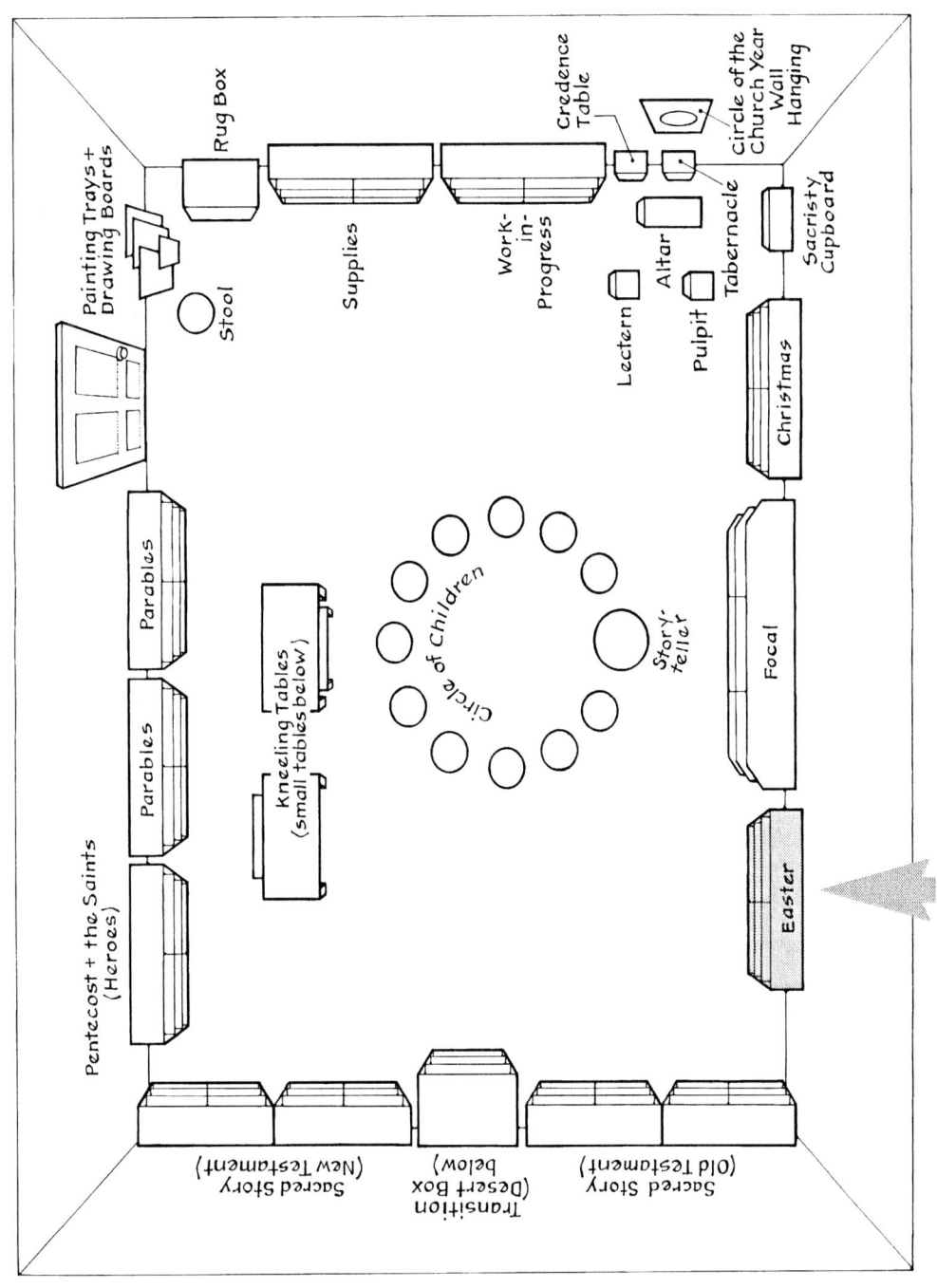

WHERE TO FIND MATERIALS

MOVEMENTS	**WORDS**
Go to the Easter shelves and bring the tray with the bag on it. Put the tray at your side and place the bag in the middle of the circle. Unless you have a rug larger than the assembled cross, tell this lesson without a rug.	Watch carefully where I go so you will always know where to find this lesson.
Pick up the bag and explore it from the outside.	Now is the time for the color purple. It is the time for preparing. Purple is the color of kings. We are preparing for the coming of a king and his going and his coming again. We are preparing for the Mystery of Easter.

This is a serious time. It takes many weeks to get ready to enter the Mystery of Easter. Let's look inside to see how many weeks it takes and what Lent makes when it is all put together. |
Place the bag back on the floor and reach inside. Pull out the first piece with the purple side up. Place it beside the bag. Turn it this way and that.	I wonder what this could be?
Encourage the children's guesses, then reach inside the bag and take out a second piece.	Look. Here is a second piece. I wonder what this could be?
Place the second piece on the floor, apart from the first piece. Turn the pieces, but do not fit them together.	
Take out the third piece. Put the third piece beside the other two, but do not fit the pieces together. Move the pieces around and try combinations that do not work.	Look. Here's a third piece. They are all so different.
Take out the fourth piece. Put the fourth piece beside the other three, but do not fit the pieces together.	Here is a fourth piece. One, two, three, four weeks in Lent? That's the same as the time for getting ready for Christmas. Perhaps that is all we need for Easter, too.
Take out the fifth piece.	Oh, no! Here's another one. Lent is longer than Advent. The Mystery of Easter is an even greater mystery than the Mystery of Christmas, so it must take longer to get ready.

MOVEMENTS	WORDS
Touch the almost empty bag and "find" yet another piece.	That must be all there is. No. It is not empty. There must be another week inside.
Take out the sixth piece.	There *is* another one! The time of Lent is six weeks. Easter is a huge mystery. Let's see if there is another one.

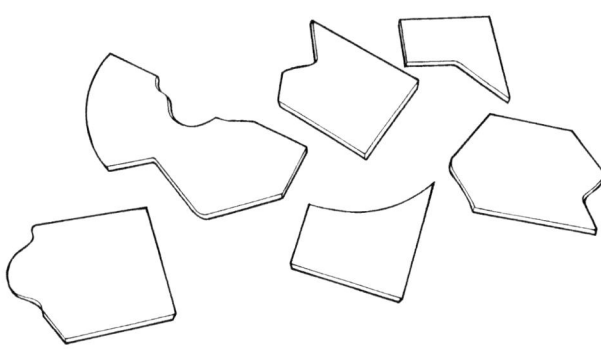

THE PIECES OF THE CROSS PUZZLE

Look in the bag. It is now empty. Place the bag on the floor and sit back to wonder about it.	Lent helps us to get ready. It is a time to know more about the One who is Easter. It is also a time to learn more about who we really are.
Touch one or more of the pieces as you talk about them.	The pieces are very purple. The One who is coming is very important, like a king. But purple can feel kind of sad, too. Perhaps what is going to happen is sad.
Begin to move the pieces around, but do not yet fit them together. Experiment. Propose alternative constructions. Play.	I wonder what all these make when you put them all together?
Finally, assemble the cross.	Oh, I see. It makes the cross, a serious cross. It is also sad. Jesus grew up to be a man and died on the cross. That *is* sad, but it is also wonderful.
	Now look what happens.
Turn the pieces over to make a completely white cross.	Jesus died on the cross, but somehow he is still with us. That is why Easter is not just sad. It is also wonderful.
Show the purple side of a few pieces.	Lent is sad...
Turn the pieces back to white again.	...Easter is pure celebration.

Godly Play   *The Mystery of Easter*   93

MOVEMENTS

WORDS

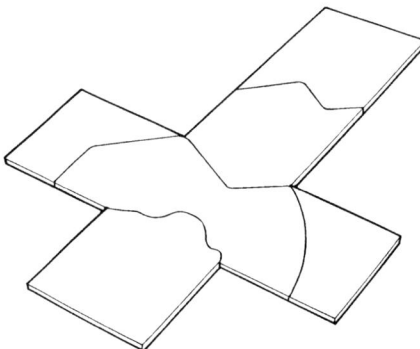

THE ASSEMBLED CROSS (STORYTELLER'S PERSPECTIVE)

Reach inside the purple bag and take hold of the inside. Turn the bag inside out.

Easter turns everything inside out and upside down. The color of getting ready becomes the color of pure celebration. The sad seriousness and happiness join together to make joy.

Count the white pieces.

Look! You can't keep Easter in just one Sunday! It goes on for one, two, three, four, five, six weeks! All the way to Pentecost.

Sit back and contemplate the Mystery of Easter for a few moments, and then begin the wondering questions.

Now I wonder if you have ever seen these colors in the church?

I wonder what happens when you see these colors?

I wonder what part of Lent you like best?

I wonder what part of Lent is the most important?

I wonder who takes care of the colors?

I wonder where these colors are when you don't see them?

I wonder if you see the white at some other time in church?

I wonder how sadness and happiness can make joy?

I wonder where joy comes from?

I wonder how you know when joy is here?

When the wondering is finished, put the pieces of the cross inside the bag, leaving it with the white on the outside. Return the material to the shelf and help the children begin to get out their work.

THE COMPLETE GUIDE TO GODLY PLAY

BY JEROME W. BERRYMAN

An imaginative method for presenting scripture stories to children

This five-volume series invites preschool through 6th-grade children to discover God, themselves and one another through our sacred stories. Based on Jerome Berryman's work in the Montessori tradition, *Godly Play* uses a careful telling of scripture stories, engaging story figures and activities to encourage children to seek and find answers to their faith questions. *Godly Play* respects the innate spirituality of children and encourages curiosity and imagination in experiencing the mystery and joy of God.

HERE'S WHAT YOU GET IN EACH VOLUME:

- **VOLUME 1: How to Lead *Godly Play* Lessons** contains all of the material you will need to be familiar with the *Godly Play* approach, including how to create a special space for children, plan and present the lesson and help children develop spiritually. 1-889108-95-2

- **VOLUME 2: Fall** - an opening lesson on the church year followed by 13 Old Testament stories, from Creation through the prophets. 1-889108-96-0

- **VOLUME 3: Winter** - includes 20 presentations based on stories about Advent and the feasts of Christmas & Epiphany, followed by the parables. 1-889108-97-9

- **VOLUME 4: Spring** - presents 20 lessons covering stories of Lent, the resurrection, the eucharist and the early Church during Easter Season. 1-889108-98-7

- **VOLUME 5: Practical Helps from Godly Play Trainers** - experienced trainers and teachers share insights, stories and ideas for using *Godly Play* to its fullest. 1-931960-04-6

HOW-TO VIDEOS

Masterful *Godly Play* storyteller Jerome W. Berryman guides catechists through two actual *Godly Play* sessions per season. In this three-part series, listeners are enthusiastically engaged in how to tell the story and invite children to experience the wondering.

Available in VHS & DVD formats

To purchase these products at 25% OFF, call Living the Good News TODAY at 1-800-824-1813.

(Mention offer SPGP.)

This offer valid for 30 days after training event.

THE COMPLETE GUIDE TO GODLY PLAY	
VOLUMES 1-5	**$ 24.95 each**

Sessions are adaptable from 45 minutes to 2 hours and include a complete materials list. 8 1/4" x 10 3/4", 120 pages, paperback

FALL VHS OR DVD	$ 24.95 each
WINTER VHS OR DVD	$ 24.95 each
SPRING VHS OR DVD	$ 24.95 each

Approximately 45 min. each.